# SCOTLAND

C000276971

| | |
|---|---|
| Key to Map Pages | 2-3 Town Plans |
| Road Maps | 4-101 Index to Towns & Villages |

## REFERENCE

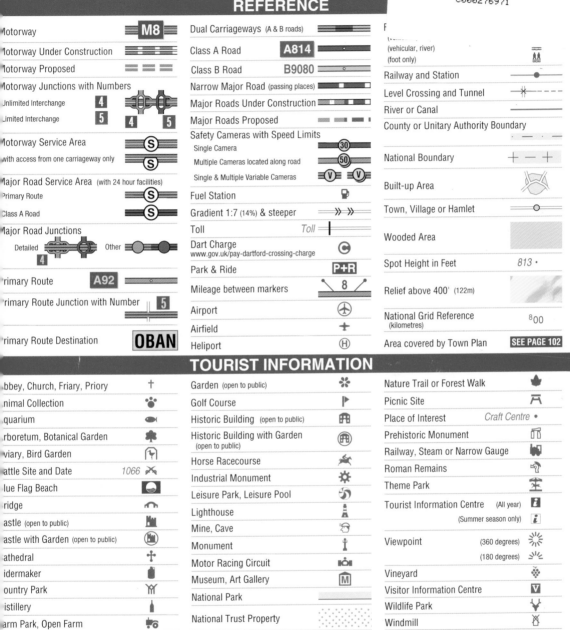

Motorway — **M8**

Motorway Under Construction

Motorway Proposed

Motorway Junctions with Numbers

Unlimited Interchange — **4**

Limited Interchange — **5**

Motorway Service Area — **S**

with access from one carriageway only — **S**

Major Road Service Area (with 24 hour facilities)

Primary Route — **S**

Class A Road — **S**

Major Road Junctions

Detailed — **4**    Other

Primary Route — **A92**

Primary Route Junction with Number — **5**

Primary Route Destination — **OBAN**

Dual Carriageways (A & B roads)

Class A Road — **A814**

Class B Road — **B9080**

Narrow Major Road (passing places)

Major Roads Under Construction

Major Roads Proposed

Safety Cameras with Speed Limits

Single Camera — **30**

Multiple Cameras located along road — **50**

Single & Multiple Variable Cameras — **V** **V**

Fuel Station

Gradient 1:7 (14%) & steeper — » »

Toll — *Toll*

Dart Charge — **C**
www.gov.uk/pay-dartford-crossing-charge

Park & Ride — **P+R**

Mileage between markers — 8

Airport — ⊕

Airfield — +

Heliport — **H**

Footpath
(vehicular, river)
(foot only)

Railway and Station

Level Crossing and Tunnel

River or Canal

County or Unitary Authority Boundary

National Boundary

Built-up Area

Town, Village or Hamlet

Wooded Area

Spot Height in Feet — 813 ·

Relief above 400' (122m)

National Grid Reference (kilometres) — 800

Area covered by Town Plan — **SEE PAGE 102**

## TOURIST INFORMATION

Abbey, Church, Friary, Priory — †

Animal Collection

Aquarium

Arboretum, Botanical Garden

Aviary, Bird Garden

Battle Site and Date — 1066

Blue Flag Beach

Bridge

Castle (open to public)

Castle with Garden (open to public)

Cathedral — ✝

Cidermaker

Country Park

Distillery

Farm Park, Open Farm

Fortress, Hill Fort

Garden (open to public)

Golf Course

Historic Building (open to public)

Historic Building with Garden (open to public)

Horse Racecourse

Industrial Monument

Leisure Park, Leisure Pool

Lighthouse

Mine, Cave

Monument

Motor Racing Circuit

Museum, Art Gallery — **M**

National Park

National Trust Property

Nature Reserve or Bird Sanctuary

Nature Trail or Forest Walk

Picnic Site

Place of Interest — *Craft Centre* •

Prehistoric Monument

Railway, Steam or Narrow Gauge

Roman Remains

Theme Park

Tourist Information Centre (All year) — **i**

(Summer season only) — **i**

Viewpoint (360 degrees)

(180 degrees)

Vineyard

Visitor Information Centre — **V**

Wildlife Park

Windmill

Zoo or Safari Park

## SCALE

| 0 | 1 | 2 | 3 | 4 | 5 | | 10 miles |
|---|---|---|---|---|---|---|---|
| 0 | 1 2 3 4 5 | | | | 10 | | 16 kilometres |

Map Pages 4-90
1:221,760
3.5 miles to 1 inch

EDITION 1 2017
Copyright © Geographers' A-Z Map Co. Ltd.
Telephone: 01732 781000 (Enquires & Trade Sales)
01732 783422 (Retail Sales)

Contains Ordnance Survey data © Crown copyright and database right 2016
Safety camera & fuel station locations supplied by www.PocketGPSworld.com Copyright 2016 © PocketGPSworld.com
Base Relief by Geo-Innovations, © www.geoinnovations.co.uk
The Shopmobility logo is a registered symbol of The National Federation of Shopmobility.

**A-Z**
A-Z Az AtoZ
registered trade marks of
Geographers' A-Z Map Company Ltd
www./az.co.uk

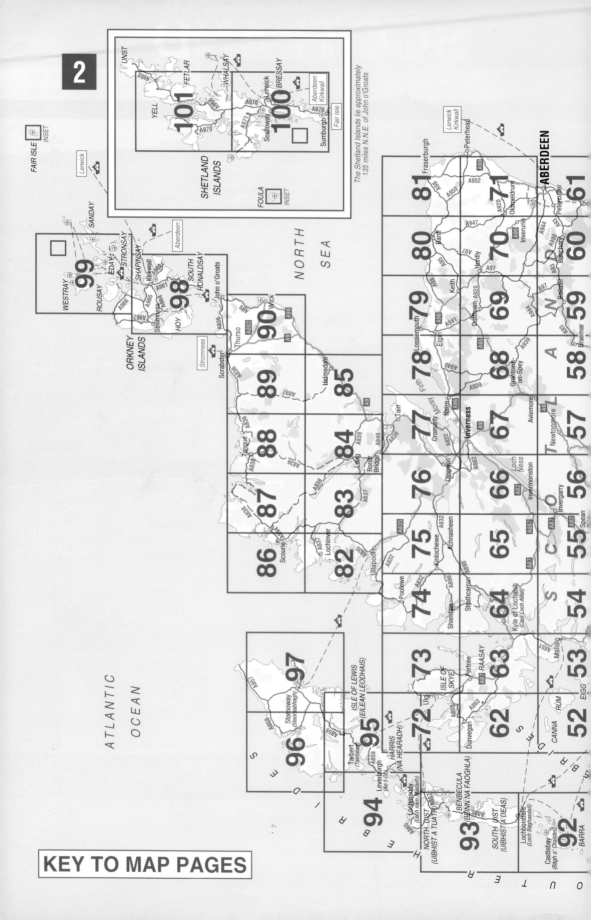

**2**

KEY TO MAP PAGES

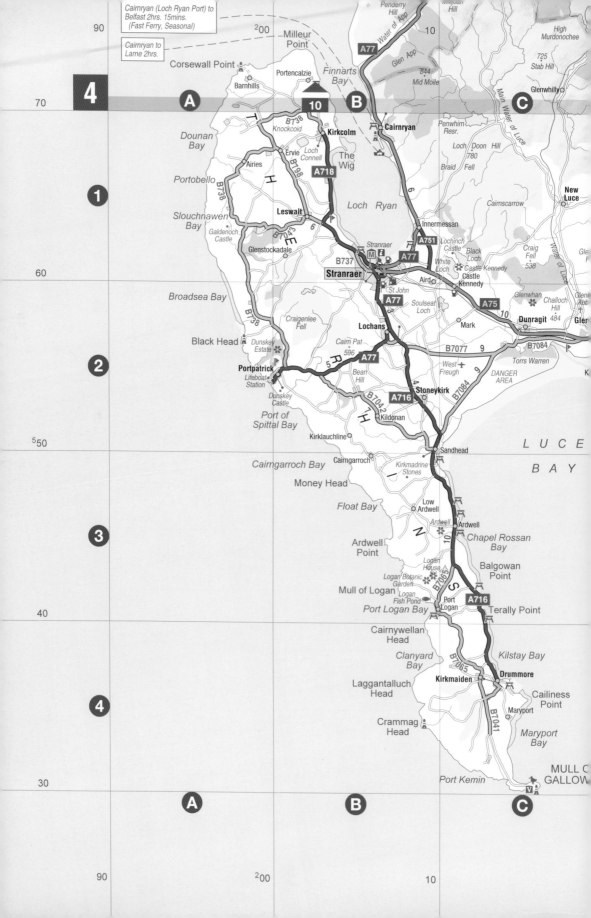

90

200

10

A

18

B

C

10

M

Tur
C

Turnberry Ba

1

Matthew's Po

600

1109
Ailsa Craig

**Girvan**
McKechnie
Institute
**Glendoune**

Woodland Bay

2

Byne
Hill
60

**A714**

13

60

Grey Hill
975

90

Straid

**Lendalfoot**

853
Knockdaw
Hill

**A77**

Poundland

Bennane
Head

**Colmonell**

B734

3

Ballantrae Bay

Knockdolian

Pinw
H

B734

Knockdolian

Heronsford

Knockdhu
756

**Ballantrae**

Water of Tig

Garleffin

Downan Point

80

1041

Strawarren
Fell

Cairnryan (Loch Ryan Port) to
Belfast 2hrs. 15mins.
(Fast Ferry, Seasonal)

Low
Ballochdowan

Currarie Port

Beneraird
1439

1046
Carlock
Hill

Cairnryan to
Larne 2hrs.

1321
Milljoan
Hill

Penderry
Hill

High
Murdonochee

4

**A77**

Water of App

Milleur
Point

725
Stab Hill

Corsewall Point

Glen App

Finnarts
Bay

844
Mid Moile

Glenwhilly

Portencalzie

Barnhills

70

Main Water

Penwhim
Resr.

A

BT

4

B

Cairnryan

C

**Dounan
Bay**

Knockcoid

**Kirkcol**

Loch
Doon Hill
780

Ervie

Loch
Connell

New
Luce

Airies

B198

The
Wig

Braid
Fell

**Portobello**

B738

**A718**

200

90

Loch Ryan

10

Cairnscarrow

New
Luce

**Slouchnawen
Bay**

6

**Leswalt**

Galdenoch

Innermessan

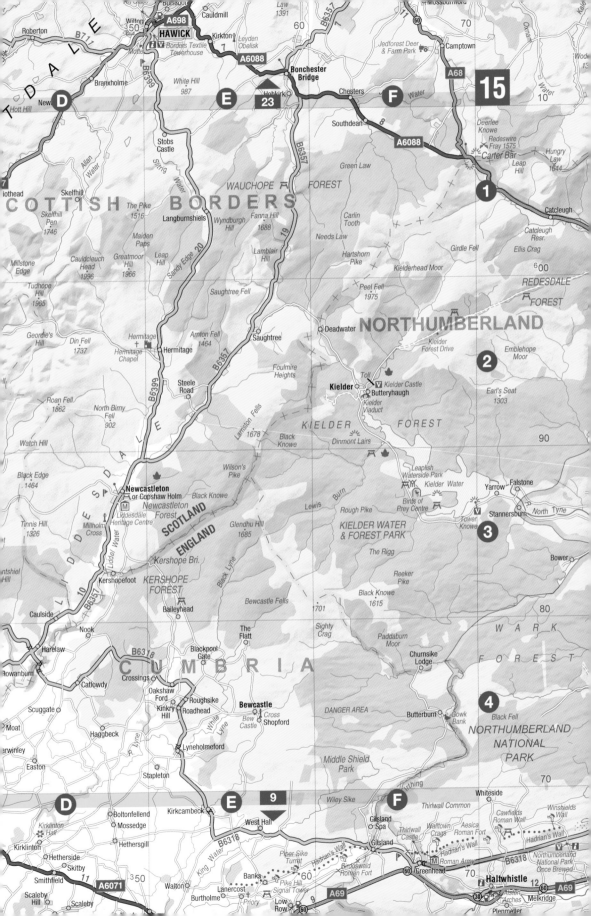

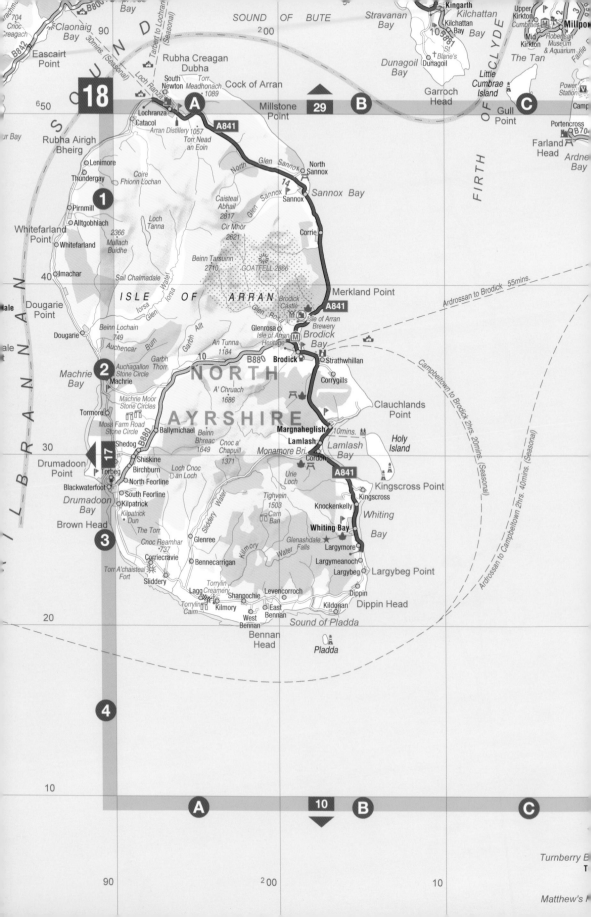

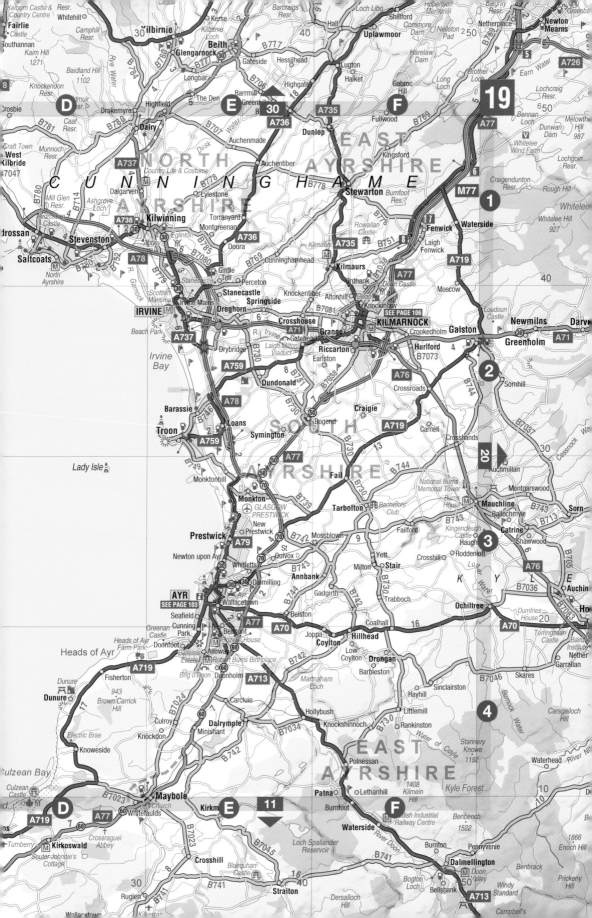

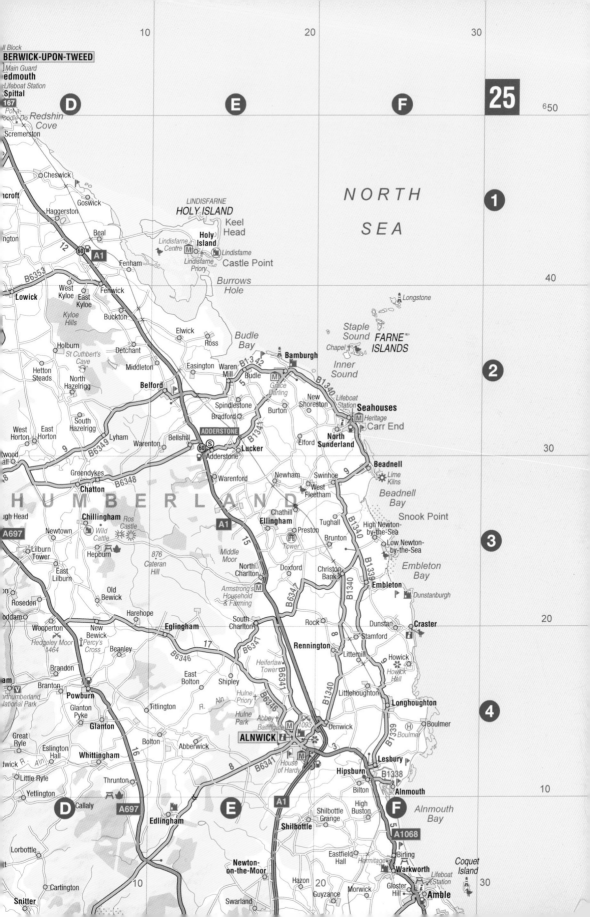

NORTH SEA

**BERWICK-UPON-TWEED**
ill Block
Main Guard
edmouth
Lifeboat Station
Spittal
167

**D**   **E**   **F**

Redshin Cove
Scremerston
Poisa
odle Do

Cheswick
Goswick
ncroft
Haggerston

LINDISFARNE
**HOLY ISLAND**
Keel Head

Beal
12   60   A1
Fenham

Lindisfarne Centre
Holy Island
Lindisfarne
Lindisfarne Priory
Castle Point

Burrows Hole

West Kyloe   East Kyloe
**Lowick**
B6353
Fenwick

Kyloe Hills

Buckton

Elwick
Ross

Budle Bay

Holburn
St Cuthbert's Cave
Detchant
Middleton

Hetton Steads
North Hazelrigg

Easington
Waren Mill
Budle
**Bamburgh**
B1342

**Belford**
5

Spindlestone
Bradford
Grace Darling

Burton
New Shoreston

Longstone

Staple Sound
**FARNE ISLANDS**
Chapel
Inner Sound

**D**   **E**   **F**   **25**   650

**1**

40

**2**

30

B1340
Lifeboat Station
**Seahouses**
Heritage
Carr End

West Horton   East Horton
South Hazelrigg
B6349
Lyham
Warenton
Bellshill

**ADDERSTONE**
60 S
Adderstone
**Lucker**

Elford
**North Sunderland**

wood all
9

Greendykes
B6348
**Chatton**

Warenford

Newham
Swinhoe
9
**Beadnell**
Lime Kilns

gh Head

Newtown
**Chillingham**
Ros Castle
Wild Cattle
Hepburn

West Fleetham
Chathill
**Ellingham**
Preston Tower
Brunton

Beadnell Bay

Snook Point

High Newton-by-the-Sea

**3**

**HUMBERLAND**

A697
Lilburn Tower
East Lilburn

876
Cateran Hill

A1

Middle Moor
North Charlton
15

Doxford

Tughall

Low Newton-by-the-Sea

Embleton Bay

Roseden
oddam

Old Bewick
Harehope

Armstrong's Household & Farming
M

South Charlton

Rock

Christon Bank
B6347

**Embleton**
B1340
Dunstanburgh

Wooperton
Hedgeley Moor 1464
New Bewick
Percy's Cross
Beanley

Eglingham
B6346
17

East Bolton
Shipley
B6341

Aln R.

Heiferlaw Tower
B6341

**Rennington**

Dunstan
**Craster**
Stamford

Littlemill

Howick
Howick Hall

20

am
V
Branton
**Powburn**

Brandon

Glanton Pyke
**Glanton**

Titlington

Abberwick

Hulne Priory
Hulne Park
Abbey
Bailiffgate M
1093

**ALNWICK**

Denwick

Littlehoughton

**Longhoughton**
B1339
Boulmer
H
Boulmer

**4**

10

northumberland ational Park

Great Ryle
Eslington Hall

Whittingham
16

Bolton

Thrunton

Bolton

House of Hardy
M
B6341
3

Lesbury
B1338

Hipsburn
Bilton
**Alnmouth**

wick
Aln R.
Little Ryle
Yetlington

Callaly
A697

Edlingham

**D**   **E**   **F**

Shilbottle Grange
**Shilbottle**

High Buston

Alnmouth Bay

A1

A1068

Lorbottle
Cartington

**Snitter**

**Newton-on-the-Moor**

Hazon
20
Guyzance
Morwick

Swarland

Eastfield Hall
Hermitage
Gloster Hill

Birling
**Warkworth**
Lifeboat Station

Coquet Island

30

**Amble**

100    10    20

90    **26**    Ⓐ    Ⓑ    Ⓒ

❶

80

❷

Nave Is

Eilean
Beag

Ardnave
Loch

70    Tòn Mhór    Loch
Laingeadail    Kilnave

Loch Còrr    Sanaigmore    Loch an
Rubha    Braigo    Fhir Mhór
Lamanais    Grulinbeg    Leckgruinart

Saligo Bay    Loch Gorm    B8017    G

Saligo    Castle    S
B8018

Coul
Point    7

Distillery    A

Machir    Kilchoman    Conisby    Carra
Bay    Cnoc Dubh    Dhu

Distillery    Bruichladdic

60    Kilchiaran    Loch
Kilchiaran    Gearach    Islay
Bay    Life

Octomore    V

Cultoon    Natural History
Stone Circle    Port    Centre
Lossit    Beinn Tart    Charlotte
a' Mhill
760

Lossit    Neribus
Bay    Lagg

❹    Octofad    Laggan
Point

Portnahaven    A847    Port Gleann    Lagg
na Gaoidh
Orsay    Port Wemyss    Ba

⁶50    RHINNS POINT    Ⓐ    Ⓑ    Ⓒ

Slugaide
Glas

100    10    20    Gle
Dùn Mór Ghil

**ISLE OF JURA**

**PAPS OF JURA**

**JURA FOREST**

**SOUND OF JURA**

**ISLE OF GIGHA**

**ARGYLL & BUTE**

**ORONSAY**

Colonsay to Port Askaig 1hr. 10mins. (Seasonal)

Craighouse to Tayvallich 1hr. (Seasonal)

Kennacraig to Port Askaig 2hrs.

Kennacraig to Port Ellen 2hrs. 20mins.

Glendebadel Bay 60

Loch Doire na h-Achlaise

Ben Garrisdale 1198

Lochanan Tana

Cruach Ionnastail 967

Loch Fada Cul na Beinne

Ardlussa

Inverlussa

Lussa Point

Gob Dubh

Lussa River 90

Beinn an Oir 153?

Maol nam Damh 887

Loch Cathar nan Eun

Corpach Bay

Fishing Loch

Lealt

Shian Bay

Allt an Tairbh

Rainberg Mór 1487

Dubh Bheinn

Shian River

Loch an Tuim Uaine

Loch Righ Mòr

Cruib 1036

622 Beinn Sgaillinish

Loch Righ Beag

Loch Lùbanach

Tarbert

Rubh'an t-Sailein

Loch Tarbert

Loch an Aircill

Cnoc an Ime 927

A846 80

Rubh' a' chrois-aoinidh

Lochan Maol an t-sornaich

Allt na Gile

Glen Batrick

Beinn Bhreac 1439

Lagg 16

Loch Lesgamaill

Post Rocks

**RUBHA A'MHAIL**

Rubha Bholsa

Sgarbh Breac 1195

Bachlaig

Loch an Oir

Beinn an Oir 2576

Loch a' Chnuic Bhric

2477

Loch na Fudarlaich

Corran

Port Doir' a' Chrorain

Eilean Mòr

Sgairinn

Sgarbh Dubh 965

Loch Smigeadail

Distillery

Bunnahabhain

Ardnahoe

Loch Staoisha Distillery

Lochan Gleann Astaile

Astaile

Glas Bheinn 1839

Loch an t-Siob

An Dùnan

Skervuile

Beinn Bhreac 940

Giur-bheinn 1037

Giur-bheinn

Gleann Iubharnadeal

Knockrome

Ardfernal

Gortantaoid

Sgarrail

Sgarbh Dubh

Caol Ila

Gleann

Leargybreck

Jura

Loch na Mile

Keills

Port Askaig (Port Asgaig)

Feolin Ferry

Loch Allan

Loch a' Bhaile-Mhargaidh

Isle of Jura Distillery

Keils

Small Isles

Finlaggan

Loch Finlaggan

A846

Loch Ballygrant

Gleann Ullibh

Craighouse

Ballygrant 8

Loch Lossit

1123 Brat Bheinn

Port na Birlinne

Loch Leathan

Loch Cam

Kilmeny

Beinn Dubh 875

Cabrach

A846

Loch Drolsay

Islay Ales Brewery

Esknish

R. Sorn

Glas Eilean

8

Ardfin

Na Cùiltean

Redhouses

Woolen Mill

Loch Bharradail

Am Fraoch Eilean

Rubha na Tràille

Carnain

Bridgend (Beul an Atha)

Dun Nosebridge Hillfort

Brosdale Island

Glas Bheinn 1544

McArthur's Head

Bowmore

B8016

Mulindry

Loch Allallaidh

An Dubh

3 Church

Beinn Bhàn 1544

Beinn Bheigeir 1612

Carraig Mhór

Eilean Garbh

West Tarbert Bay

Laggan Bri.

Kilennan River

Claggan River

Ardtalla

Laggan River

Loch nan Breac 1490

Beinn Uraraidh

Claggain Bay

ISLE OF GIGHA

Torra

Loch Beinn Uraraidh

Loch Leathann an Sgorra

354 Cnoc Mòr na Claigin

Aros Bay

Creag han 33?

Glenegedale Lots

Kintour

Ardmore Point

Ardminish

Mill Loch

Beinn Sholum 1138

Loch Carn a' Mhaoil

Kildalton Cross

Craobhach

Ardminish Bay

Leorin Lochs

Loch Uigeadail

Craro Island

Kintra

Loch nan Gabhar

Loch Sholum

Loch Iarnan

Eilean Bhride

650

Loch Muchairt

A846

Loch a' Chnuic

Eilean a' Chuirn

Gigalum Island

Cragabus

Lagavulin Distillery

Laphroaig Distillery

Ardbeg Distillery

Dunyvaig Castle

Rubha na Gainmhich

Eilean Imersay

Cara Island

Port Ellen

Texa

150

60

27

1

2

3

4

36

28

16

Staffa
Fingal's Cave

Little Colonsay

Inch Kenneth
Chapel

B8035
17
Derry 50

Glen

BEN MORE
3171

Corra-bheinn
2311

Gribun

Coirc Bheinn
1837

Erisgeir

Beinn na Sreine 1704

ARDMEANACH

B8035

Coladoir River

Réidh Eilean

Eilean Annraidh
Abbey & Nunnery

Creag Bheinn 1613
MacCulloch's Fossil-Tree

Tiroran

Kilfinichen Bay

Sailisdea

Loch Fuaran

Rubha na h Uamha

Tavool House

Port na Croise

Scridain

Pennyghael

Beinn na Croise 1649

Maclean's Cross
Iona Heritage

Rubha nan Cearc

Garbh Phort

Kintra
Creich
Columba Centre
Aridhglas

Eorabus

Loch an Leòib

Ardchrishnish

A849 Torrans

Leidle River

91

IONA

70mins

Baile Mór

Stac an Aoineidh

Eilean nah-Aon Chaorach

Sound of Iona

Fionnphort

Loch Poit na h-I

A849

Loch na Làthaich

Knockan

12

BROLASS

Beinn Chreagach 1235

Carsaig

Fidden

Beinn a' Ghlinne Mhoir
369 Ross of Mull Historical Centre

Bunessan
Loch Assopol

Beach River

Carsaig Arches

Carsaig Bay

Greave
20

Erraid

Knockvologan

Ardalanish

Uisken

Cruachan Min 1232

Aoineadh Mòr

Malcolm's Point

Soa Island

Eilean nam Muc

Beinn a' Chaol-Airigh 411

Ardchiavaig

Rubha nam Bràithrean

Eilean a' Chalmain

Ardalanish Bay

2

Rubh' Ardalanish

West Reef

Torran Rocks

Sgeir Dhoirbh

10

F I R T H

3

Oban to Colonsay 2hrs 20mins

7 00

Port na Cuilce

Balnahard

Kiloran Bay

Uragaig
Loch an Sgoltaire
Kiloran

.469 Carnan Eoin

Port Ceann a' Gharraidh

B8086 Colonsay House

COLONSAY

Port a' Bhàta

Sgreadan

4

Kilchattan

B8086

Loch Fada 4

B8085

3

Glas Aird

Scalasaig

Eilean a' Chladaich

Colonsay

Loch Staosnaig

Corpach Bay

Garvard

B8085

Eilean Leathann

Rubha Dubh

90

C

Dubh Eilean

Oronsay

ORONSAY

Colonsay to Port Askaig 1hr. 10mins (Seasonal)

Dubh Tairbh
Rainberg Mòr 1487

Shian Bay

Caolas Mòr

Eilean Ghaoideamal

Loch an Tuim Uaine

Shian River

Loch Chr

Eilean nan Ron

Ceann Riobha

30

40

150

Loch Righ Mòr

Cruib 1036

Loch Righ Beag

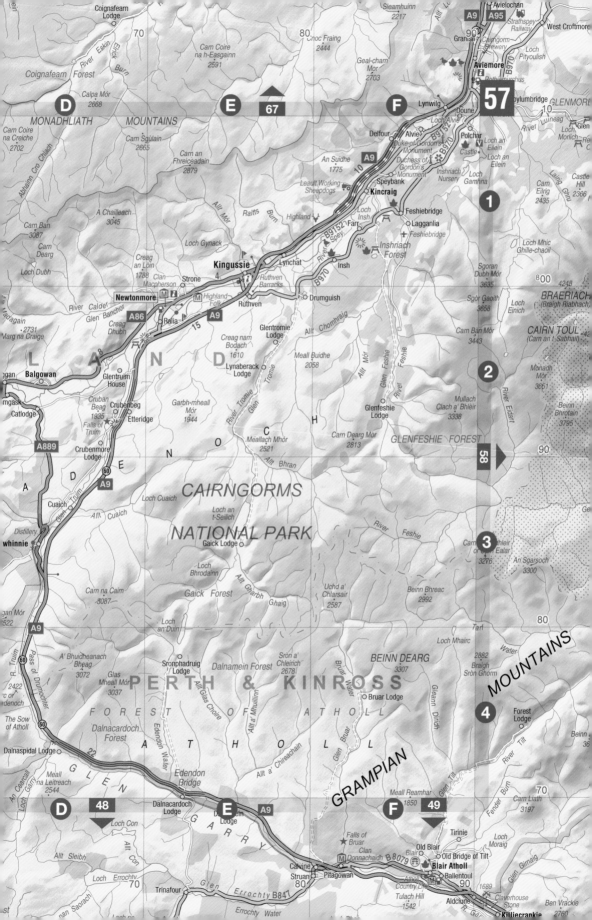

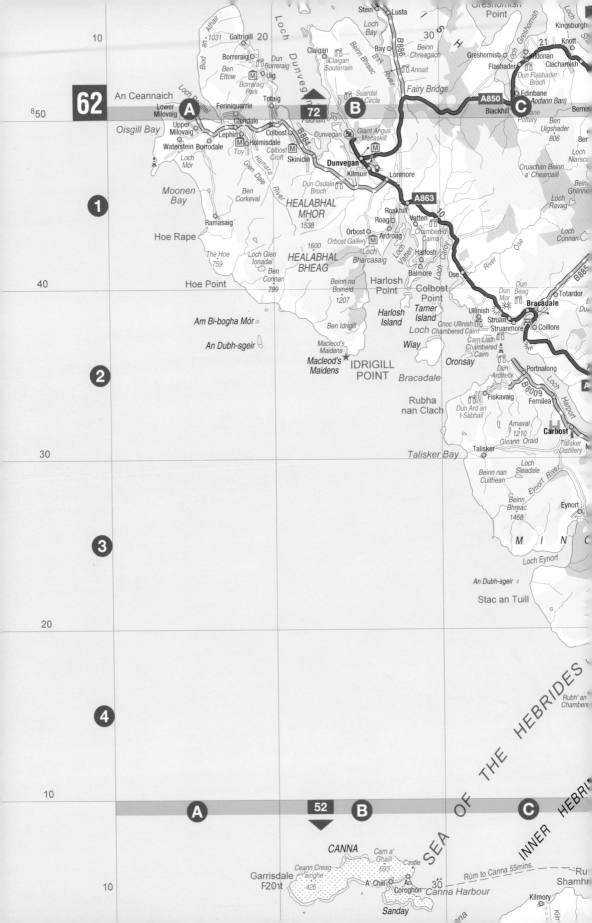

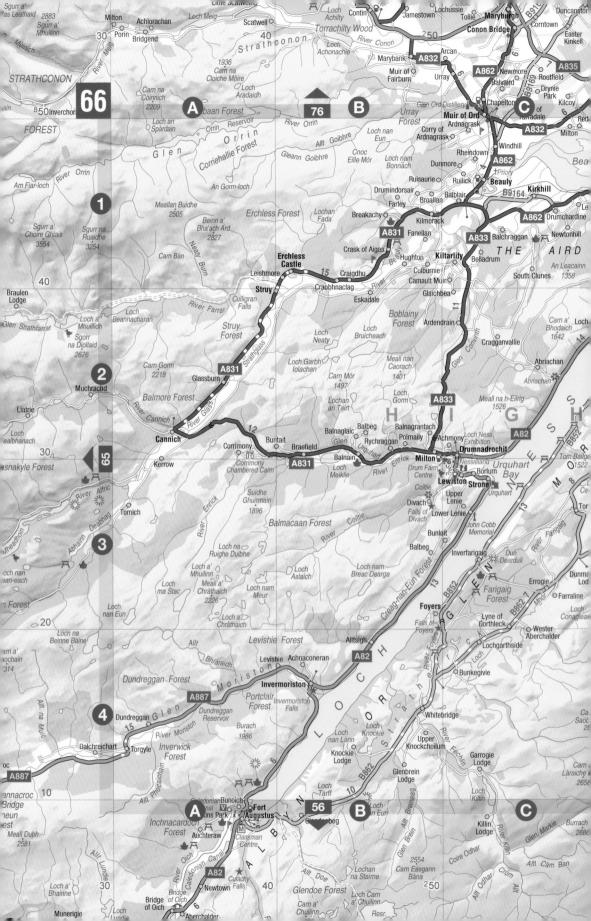

A859

Seileboist

Miabhag

Scalpaigh

SCALPAY
(Scalpaigh)

Loch An
Tairbh'Uirt

Ceann a
Bhaigh

Eilean Glas

30

An Coileach
1267

Ceann a
Bhaigh

Aird
Mhighe

Drinisiadar

Ceann-na-Cleithe

Greosabhagh

Plocrapol

Harris Tweed
and Knitwear

Scadabhagh

SOUTH HARRIS
(n a Deas na Hearadh)

72

Liceasto

Leac a Li

Caolas
Stocinis

Geocrab

Rubha
Bhocaig

B

C

I

Beacrabhaic

Gollam

Aird
Shleibhe

Eilean
Stocinis

Manais

A

Fleoideabhagh

Loch
Fhleoideabhaigh

Aird
Mhighe

Cuidhtinis

Tarbert to
Uig 1hr. 40mins.

Fionnsabhagh

359

Ceann a
Bhaigh

Rubha
Chuidhtinis

1

Lingreabhagh

Eilean
Lingreabhagh

Rodel

Bhalaigh

80

Sgeir nam M

Fladda-chùain

95

2

An t-Iasgair

Lùb S

Camas Mór

Hungladder

70

Bornesketaig
(Borgh na Sgiotaig)

Kilmuir

WATERNISH
POINT

Uig to
Tarbert 1hr. 40mins.

Dùn Liath

Balgown

A855

Linicro
(Lionacro)

Totscore

Uig to
Lochmaddy 1hr. 40mins.

Eilean
Iosal

Eilean
Creagach

Dun
Skudiburgh

3

Dun Gearymore
Broch

Healaval

Dun Borrafiach
Broch

Ascrib
Islands

Idrigill

Standi
Ston

W

931

Geary

LOCH

SNIZORT

60

Ardmore
Point

The Trial
Stone

Ben Geary

Church

Knockbreck

Uig Bay

Earlish
(Earlais)

Trumpan

Halistra

Loch Losait

HIGHL

Hallin

Gillen

Mingay

Dun
Hallin

Score
Horan

A87

DUNVEGAN
HEAD

Isay

Sgeir
nam Biast

Skyeskyns

Beinn
Chamach Bheag

Lyndale
Point

Eilean Mór

Greshornish
Point

Stein

Lusta

Kingsburgh

4

Galtrigill

Loch
Bay

Bay

Greshornish

Knott

Blod an Athair

1031

Borreraig

Dun
Borreraig

Claigan

Claigan
Souterrain

Beinn Bhreac

Annait

Beinn
Chreagach

B886

Flashader

Kildonan

Clachamish

Dun Flashader
Broch

Ben
Ettow

Uig

Borreraig
Park

Totaig

Dun
Fiadhairt

Suardal
Hut Circle

Fairy
Bridge

Edinbane
(An t-Aodann Ban)

Bern

An Ceannaich

Loch Pooltiel

Feriniquarrie

A850

Edinbane
Pottery

Lower
Milovaig

Upper
Mil...

Blackhill

Ben
Uigshader

Oisgill Bay

A

Lephin

Glendale

Colbost

62

B

int Angus
Macaskill

C

806

Waterstein

Borrodale

Holmisdale

Toy

Colbost
Croft

Skinidin

Dunvegan

Be

Loch
Mór

Kilmuir

Lonmore

Moonen
Bay

Glen Dale

Hamara River

Dun Osdale
Broch

A863

Loch
Ravag

Ben
Corkeval

HEALABHAL
MHOR
1538

Roskhill

30

Loch
Connan

Ramasaig

Roag

Vatten

Cruachan Beinn
a' Chearcaill

Hoe Rape

Orbost

Ardroag

Chambered
Cairns

THE

LITTLE

MINCH

WESTERN

ISLES

TARBAT
NESS

Wilkhaven

GER AREA

**1** Bindal

**Portmahomack** Tarbat Discovery Centre
Seafield

Inver Rockfield

Lochslin Lower
Low Arboll Toulvaddie
Pitke 80 Tarrel

h Eye Geanies
10

**Hill of
Fearn**

Fearn

Tullich Hilton of
Cadboll-Chapel
Clach a **Hilton of
Cadboll**
Charridh **Balintore**
**2** Shandwick

Port an Righ

Nigg

70

**77**

N O R T

**Hopeman**
Well B9040 Duffus
**Burghead** **Cummingstown**
Roseisle
**Burghead Bay** Roseisle
Forest
College of
Roseisle
Quarrywood
B9089
**3** Heritage **17** Newton
Centre Findhorn
**Findhorn** Coltfield **12**
Alves
Findhorn Woodland Pa
Findhorn Gle
Foundation **Bay** D
Kinloss
Miltonduff
Culbin Forest **A96** Distillery
Kinloss Muir
**60** Cloddymoss Kintessack B9011 Abbey Miltono
Cran Loch Bonfromach Sueno's Monaughty Forest
Distillery Stone
Loch Loy **Dyke** Broom Heldon Hill Forresterseat
of Moy Nelson Tower **1046**
Rodney **FORRES** Lochaber Pluscarden
**NAIRN** Stone Brodie Balnageith Abbey **M O**
Druim Falconer Califer Barnhill
Tradespark Kingsteps Whiterow Black Burn
**A96** Dallas Dhu Pluscarden
2 Brodie Historic Distillery **Rafford** Hill of the
Moss-side Auldearn 7 Loch of Blairs Moor of Wangie **1046** Kellas
**4** Motte Granary Dallas
Foynesfield Whitemire **A940** Damhead Forest
**B9101** Blackhills Conicaval Altyre Romach **Dallas**
Muckle Burn Woods Loch Branchill
River Nairn Geddes Meikle Hill
Brackla Darnaway Forest Newtyle Forest **932** Cairn Uish
Regoul Hill of **1197**
**B9090** Laiken Forest Tomechole Glenlatterach
Piperhill **A939** Logie **1129** Reservoir
**Cawdor** Culcharry Littlemill Logie Steading Drumine Mill Buie
Urquhany Randolph's Forest **1218**
Leap Carnach
**A** Relugas **B** Loch
Dunphail Dallas
Newlands of Glenernie Loch
Fleenas Wood Redburn Noir 10 River Lossie
Clunas Loch Ferness Upper
Clunas Delvat **300** Glenferness Black Burn River Divie
Reservoir Ardclach Mains Loch Cair
Bell Tower 13
Carn a' 90 Glenferness Knockando
Mains

**68**
Dunphail
**A** **B** **C**

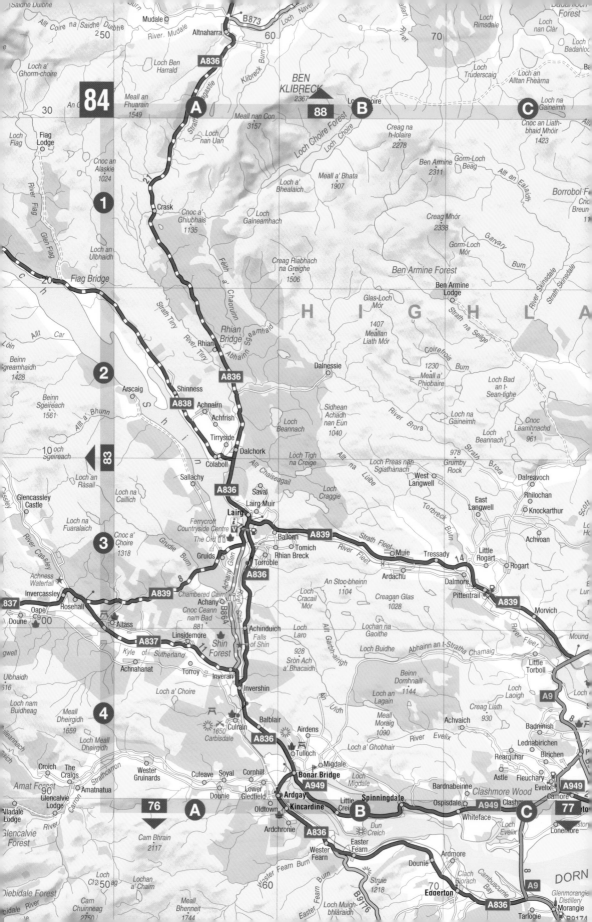

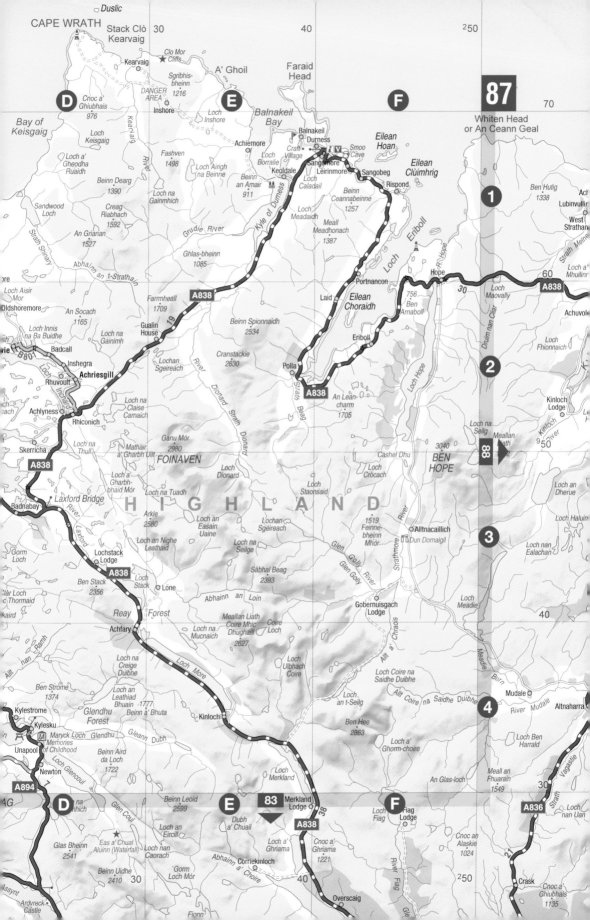

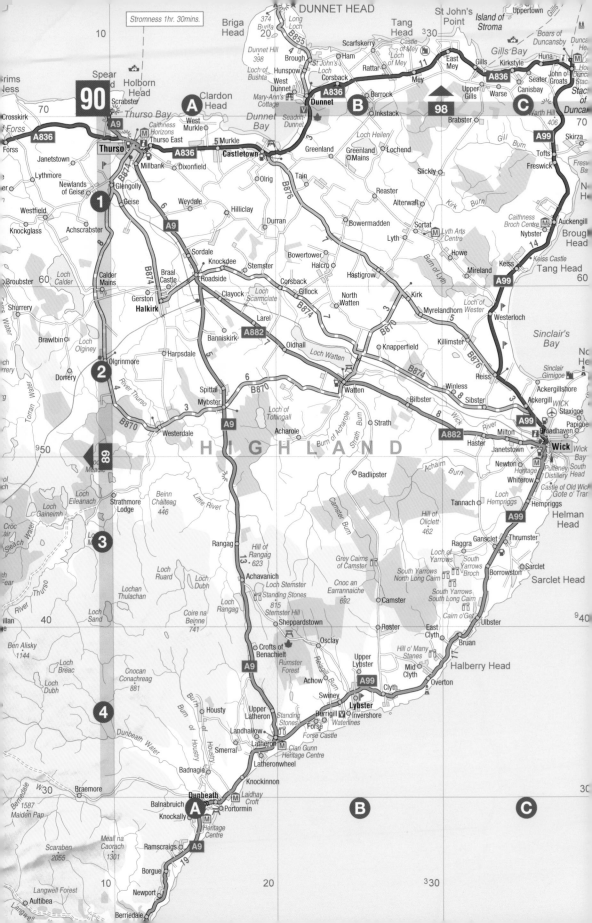

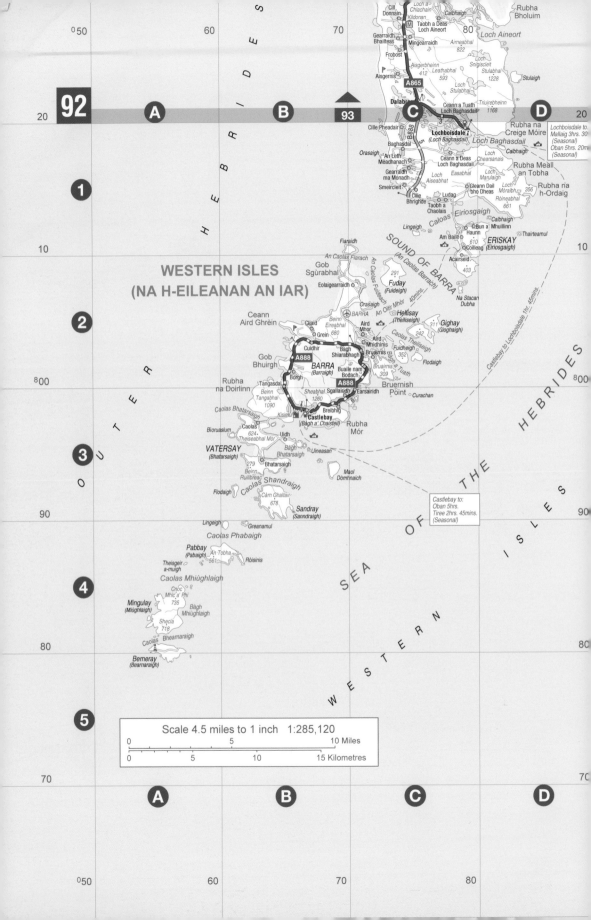

SHETLAND
ISLANDS

Scale 4.5 miles to 1 inch   1:285,120

0 | 5 | 10 Miles
0 | 5 | 10 | 15 Kilometres

SHETLAND
ISLANDS

100

# CITY & TOWN PLANS

## Reference to Town Plans

| | | | |
|---|---|---|---|
| MOTORWAY | **M8** | ABBEY, CATHEDRAL, PRIORY ETC. | † |
| MOTORWAY UNDER CONSTRUCTION | | BUS STATION | |
| MOTORWAY JUNCTIONS WITH NUMBERS | 4 5 | CAR PARK (selection of) | P |
| Unlimited Interchange 4 Limited Interchange 5 | | CHURCH | † |
| PRIMARY ROUTE | **A82** | CITY WALL | |
| DUAL CARRIAGEWAYS | | FERRY (Vehicular) | |
| CLASS A ROAD | A910 | (Foot only) | |
| CLASS B ROAD | B754 | GOLF COURSE | |
| MAJOR ROADS UNDER CONSTRUCTION | | HELIPORT | |
| MAJOR ROADS PROPOSED | | HOSPITAL | H |
| MINOR ROADS | | LIGHTHOUSE | |
| SAFETY CAMERA | 30 | MARKET | |
| FUEL STATION | | NATIONAL TRUST FOR SCOTLAND PROPERTY (Open) | NTS |
| RESTRICTED ACCESS | | (Restricted opening) | NTS |
| PEDESTRIANIZED ROAD & MAIN FOOTWAY | | PARK & RIDE | |
| ONE-WAY STREETS | | PLACE OF INTEREST | ■ |
| TOLL | TOLL | POLICE STATION | ▲ |
| RAILWAY AND STATION | | POST OFFICE | ★ |
| SUBWAY | | SHOPPING AREA (Main street and precinct) | |
| LEVEL CROSSING AND TUNNEL | | SHOPMOBILITY | |
| TRAM STOP AND ONE-WAY TRAM STOP | | TOILET | ▼ |
| BUILT-UP AREA | | TOURIST INFORMATION CENTRE | i |
| | | VIEWPOINT | |
| | | VISITOR INFORMATION CENTRE | V |

## ABERDEEN

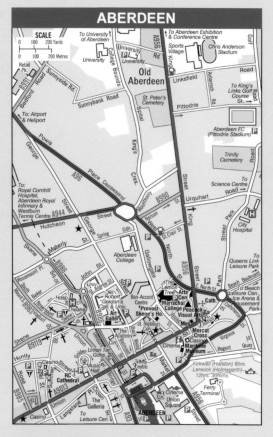

## AVIEMORE

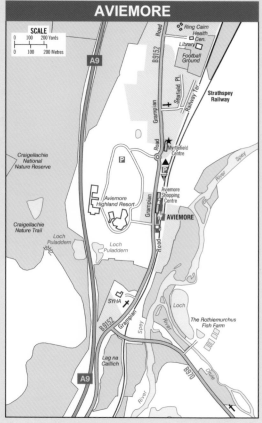

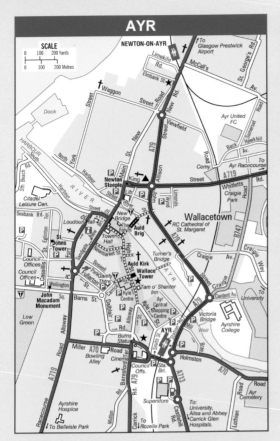

# AYR

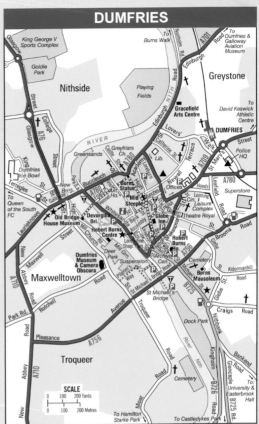

# DUMFRIES

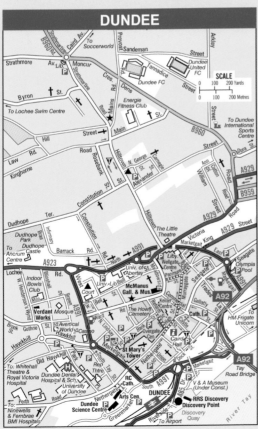

# DUNDEE

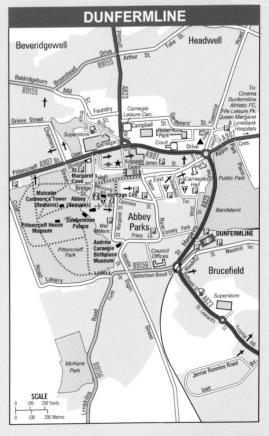

# DUNFERMLINE

# EDINBURGH

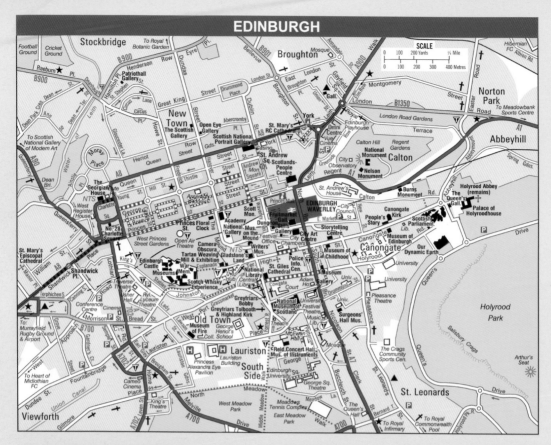

# GLASGOW

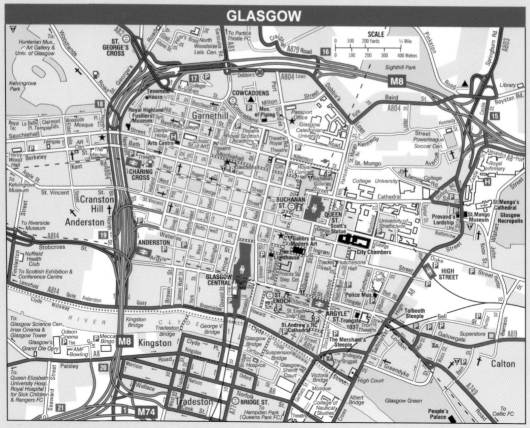

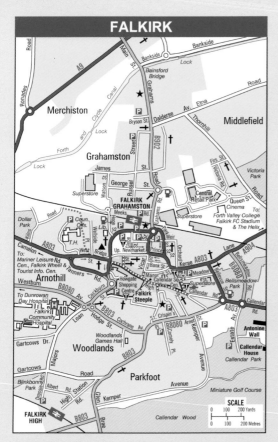

# FALKIRK

# FORT WILLIAM

# HAMILTON

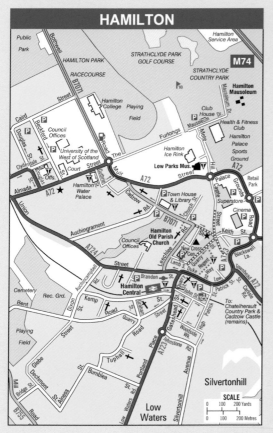

# INVERNESS

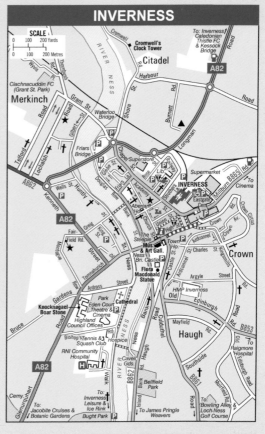

# KILMARNOCK

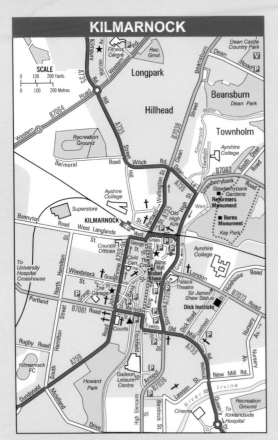

# KIRKCALDY

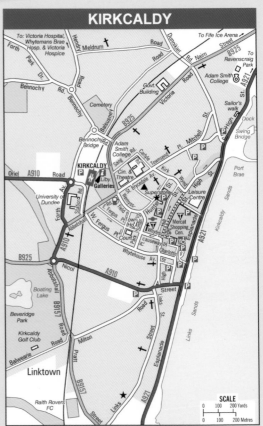

# MOTHERWELL

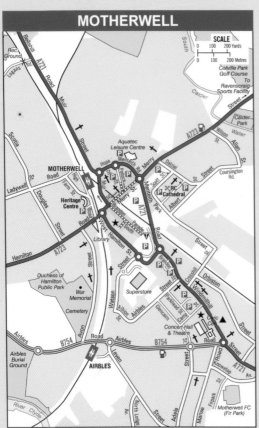

# OBAN

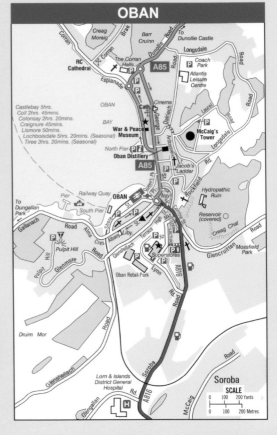

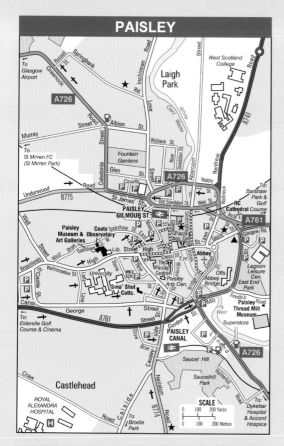

# PAISLEY

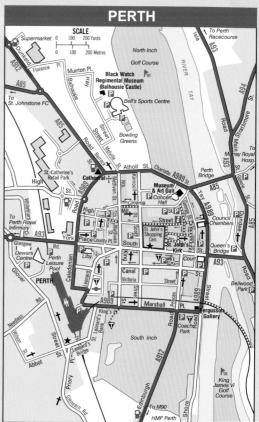

# PERTH

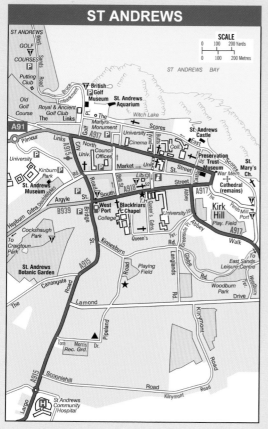

# ST ANDREWS

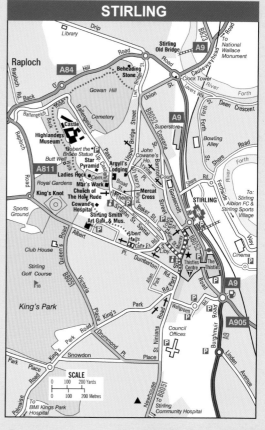

# STIRLING

# INDEX TO CITIES, TOWNS, VILLAGES, HAMLETS & LOCATIONS

(1) A strict alphabetical order is used e.g. An Gleann Ur follows Angerton but precedes Ankerville.

(2) The map reference given refers to the actual map square in which the town spot or built-up area is located and not to the place name.

(3) Only one reference is given although due to page overlaps the place may appear on more than one page.

(4) Where two places of the same name occur in the same County or Unitary Authority, the nearest large town is also given; e.g. Achiemore. *High* . . . 1E **87** (nr. Durness) indicates that Achiemore is located in square 1E on page **87** and is situated near Durness in the Unitary Authority of Highland.

(5) Major towns and destinations are shown in bold i.e. **Aberdeen.** *Aber.* . . . **102** (1E **61**). Page references for Town Plan entries are shown first.

## COUNTIES AND UNITARY AUTHORITIES with the abbreviations used in this index

Aberdeen : *Aber*
Aberdeenshire : *Abers*
Angus : *Ang*
Argyll & Bute : *Arg*
Clackmannanshire : *Clac*
Cumbria : *Cumb*
Dumfries & Galloway : *Dum*
Dundee : *D'dee*
East Ayrshire : *E Ayr*
East Dunbartonshire : *E Dun*
East Lothian : *E Lot*
East Renfrewshire : *E Ren*
Edinburgh : *Edin*
Falkirk : *Falk*
Fife : *Fife*
Glasgow : *Glas*
Highland : *High*
Inverclyde : *Inv*
Midlothian : *Midl*
Moray : *Mor*
North Ayrshire : *N Ayr*
North Lanarkshire : *N Lan*
Northumberland : *Nmbd*
Orkney : *Orkn*
Perth & Kinross : *Per*
Renfrewshire : *Ren*
Scottish Borders : *Bord*
Shetland : *Shet*
South Ayrshire : *S Ayr*
South Lanarkshire : *S Lan*
Stirling : *Stir*
West Dunbartonshire : *W Dun*
Western Isles : *W Isl*
West Lothian : *W Lot*

## A


Abberwick. Nmbd 4E 25
Abbey St Bathans. Bord 3D 35
Abbeytown. Cumb 2A 8
Aberarder. High 3D 67
Aberargie. Per 2A 42
Aberchalder. High 1A 56
Aberchirder. Abers 4B 80
Abercorn. W Lot 2C 32
Abercrombie. Fife 3E 43
Aberdalgie. Per 1F 41
**Aberdeen.** Aber 102 (1E 61)
Aberdeen International Airport. Aber 4D 71
Aberdour. Fife 1D 33
Aberfeldy. Per 3D 49
Aberfoyle. Stir 3A 40
Aberlady. E Lot 1A 34
Aberlemno. Ang 2E 51
Abernethy. Per 2A 42
Abernyte. Per 4B 50
Aberuthven. Per 2E 41
Abhainn Suidhe. W Isl 2E 95
Abington. S Lan 3E 21
Aboyne. Abers 2A 60
Abriachan. High 2C 66
Abronhill. N Lan 2F 31
Abune-the-Hill. Orkn 1A 98
Acairseid. W Isl 2C 92
Acha. Arg 2G 91
Achachork. High 1D 63
Achadh a' Chuirn. High 3F 63
Achahoish. Arg 2B 28
Achaleven. Arg 4A 46
Achallader. Arg 3E 47
Acha Mor. W Isl 4E 97
Achanalt. High 3F 75
Achandunie. High 2D 77
Ach' an Todhair. High 4D 55
Achany. High 3A 84
Achaphubuil. High 4D 55
Acharacle. High 1D 45
Acharn. Ang 4D 59
Acharn. Per 3C 48
Acharole. High 2B 90
Achateny. High 1C 44
Achavanich. High 3A 90
Achdalieu. High 4D 55
Achduart. High 3B 82
Achentoul. High 4D 89
Achfary. High 4D 87
Achfrish. High 2A 84
Achgarve. High 1B 74
Achiemore. High 1E 87 (nr. Durness)
Achiemore. High 2D 89 (nr. Thurso)
A' Chill. High 1B 52
Achiltibuie. High 3B 82
Achina. High 1C 88
Achinahuagh. High 1A 88
Achindarroch. High 2B 46
Achinduich. High 3A 84
Achinduin. Arg 4F 45
Achininver. High 1A 88
Achintee. High 1C 64
Achintraid. High 2B 64
Achleck. Arg 3B 44
Achlorachan. High 4A 76
Achluachrach. High 3F 55
Achlyness. High 2D 87
Achmelvich. High 1B 82
Achmony. High 2C 66
Achmore. High 2B 64 (nr. Stromeferry)
Achmore. High 4B 82 (nr. Ullapool)
Achnacarnin. High 4B 86
Achnacarry. High 3E 55
Achnaclerach. High 3B 76
Achnacloich. High 1E 53
Ach na Cloiche. High 1E 53
Achnaconeran. High 4B 66
Achnacroish. Arg 3F 45
Achnafalnich. Arg 1D 39
Achnagarron. High 2D 77
Achnagoul. Arg 3B 38
Achnaha. High 1B 44
Achnahanat. High 4A 84
Achnahannet. High 3A 68
Achnairn. High 2A 84
Achnamara. Arg 1B 28
Achnanellan. High 3D 55
Achnasheen. High 4E 75
Achnashellach. High 1D 65
Achosnich. High 1B 44
Achow. High 4B 90
Achranich. High 3E 45
Achreamie. High 1F 89
Achriabhach. High 1C 46
Achriesgill. High 2D 87
Achrimsdale. High 3E 85
Achscrabster. High 1F 89
Achtoty. High 1B 88
Achuvoldrach. High 2A 88
Achvaich. High 4C 84
Achvoan. High 3C 84
Ackergill. High 2C 90
Ackergillshore. High 2C 90
Adabroc. W Isl 1G 97
Adderstone. Nmbd 2E 25
Addiewell. W Lot 3B 32
Addinston. Bord 4B 34
Advie. High 2C 68
Adziel. Abers 4E 81
Ae. Dum 3E 13
Affleck. Abers 3D 71
Affric Lodge. High 3E 65
Aglionby. Cumb 2D 9
Aiginis. W Isl 3F 97
Aikers. Orkn 3C 98
Aiketgate. Cumb 3D 9
Aikhead. Cumb 3B 8
Aikton. Cumb 2B 8
Ainstable. Cumb 3E 9
Aird. Arg 3E 37
Aird. Dum 1B 4
Aird. High 2A 74 (nr. Port Henderson)
Aird. High 1E 53 (nr. Tarskavaig)
Aird. W Isl 2G 93 (on Benbecula)
Aird. W Isl 3G 97 (on Isle of Lewis)
Aird, The. High 4D 73
Àird a Bhasair. High 1F 53
Aird a Mhachair. W Isl 3G 93
Aird a Mhulaidh. W Isl 1F 95
Aird Asaig. W Isl 2F 95
Aird Dhail. W Isl 1F 97
Airdens. High 4B 84
Airdeny. Arg 1A 38
Aird Mhidhinis. W Isl 2C 92
Aird Mhighe. W Isl 3F 95 (nr. Ceann a Bhaigh)
Aird Mhighe. W Isl 4E 95 (nr. Fionnsabhagh)
Aird Mhor. W Isl 2C 92 (on Barra)
Aird Mhor. W Isl 3H 93 (on South Uist)
**Airdrie.** N Lan 3F 31
Aird Shleibhe. W Isl 4E 95
Aird Thunga. W Isl 3F 97
Aird Uig. W Isl 3B 96
Airidh a Bhruaich. W Isl 1G 95
Airies. Dum 1A 4
Airntully. Per 4F 49
Airor. High 1A 54
Airth. Falk 1B 32
Aisgernis. W Isl 5G 93
Aith. Shet 3H 101 (on Fetlar)
Aith. Shet 1B 100 (on Mainland)
Aithsetter. Shet 3C 100
Akeld. Nmbd 3C 24
Albyfield. Cumb 2E 9
Alcaig. High 4C 76
Aldclune. Per 1E 49
Aldochlay. Arg 4E 39
Aldoth. Cumb 3A 8
Alexandria. W Dun 1B 30
Alford. Abers 4A 70
Aline Lodge. W Isl 1F 95
Alladale Lodge. High 1B 76
Allanbank. N Lan 4A 32
Allanton. N Lan 4A 32
Allanton. Bord 4E 35
Allerby. Cumb 4F 7
Alligin Shuas. High 4B 74
**Alloa.** Clac 4D 41
Allonby. Cumb 3F 7
Alloway. S Ayr 4E 19
Alltgobhlach. N Ayr 1F 17
Alltnacaillich. High 3F 87
Allt na h' Airbhe. High 4C 82
Alltour. High 3F 55
Alltsigh. High 4B 66
Almondbank. Per 1F 41
Alness. High 3D 77
Alnessferry. High 3D 77
Alnham. Nmbd 4C 24
Alnmouth. Nmbd 4F 25
**Alnwick.** Nmbd 4E 25
Alston. Cumb 3F 9
Altandhu. High 2A 82
Altanduin. High 1D 85
Altass. High 3F 83
Alterwall. High 1B 90
Altgaltraig. Arg 2E 29
Altnabreac. High 3F 89
Altnacealgach. High 2D 83
Altnafeadh. High 2D 47
Altnaharra. High 4A 88
Altonhill. E Ayr 2F 19
Altrua. High 2F 55
Alva. Clac 4D 41
Alves. Mor 3C 78
Alvie. High 1F 57
Alwinton. Nmbd 4C 24
Alyth. Per 3B 50
Amatnatua. High 4F 83
Am Baile. W Isl 1C 92
Amble. Nmbd 4F 25
Amisfield. Dum 3F 13
Amulree. Per 4E 49
Anaheilt. High 1F 45
An Àird. High 1E 53
An Camus Darach. High 2F 53
An Cnoc. W Isl 3F 97
An Cnoc Ard. W Isl 1G 97
An Coroghon. High 1B 52
Ancroft. Nmbd 1D 25
Ancrum. Bord 3F 23
An Dùnan. High 3E 63
Angerton. Cumb 2B 8
An Gleann Ur. W Isl 3F 97
Ankerville. High 2F 77
An Leth Meadhanach. W Isl 1C 92
Annan. Dum 1B 8
Annat. Arg 1B 38
Annat. High 4B 74
Annathill. N Lan 2F 31
Annbank. S Ayr 3F 19
An Sailean. High 1D 45
Anston. S Lan 1F 21
Anstruther Easter. Fife 3E 43
Anstruther Wester. Fife 3E 43
An Taobh Tuath. W Isl 4D 94
An t-Aodann Ban. High 4C 72
An t Ath Leathann. High 3F 63
An Teanga. High 1F 53
Anthorn. Cumb 2A 8
An t-Ob. W Isl 4E 95
An t-Òrd. High 4F 63
Anwoth. Dum 2A 6
Appin. Arg 3A 46
Applecross. High 1A 64
Applegarthtown. Dum 3A 14
Applethwaite. Cumb 4B 8
Appletreehall. Bord 4E 23
Arabella. High 2F 77
Arasaig. High 3F 53
Arbeadie. Abers 2B 60
Arbirlot. Ang 3F 51
**Arbroath.** Ang 3F 51
Arbuthnott. Abers 4D 61
Arcan. High 4C 76
Archargary. High 2C 88
Archiestown. Mor 1D 69
Ardachu. High 3B 84
Ardalanish. Arg 2A 36
Ardaneaskan. High 2B 64
Ardarroch. High 2B 64
Ardbeg. Arg 1F 29 (nr. Dunoon)
Ardbeg. Arg 3F 16 (on Islay)
Ardbeg. Arg 3E 29 (on Isle of Bute)
Ardcharnich. High 1E 75
Ardchiavaig. Arg 2A 36
Ardchonnell. Arg 2A 38
Ardchrishnish. Arg 1B 36
Ardchronie. High 1D 77
Ardchullarie. Stir 2A 40
Ardchyle. Stir 1A 40
Ard-dhubh. High 1A 64
Ardechive. High 2E 55
Ardelve. High 3B 64
Arden. Arg 1B 30
Ardendrain. High 2C 66
Ardentinny. Arg 1F 29
Ardeonaig. Stir 4B 48
Ardersier. High 4E 77
Ardery. High 1E 45
Ardessie. High 1D 75
Ardfern. Arg 3F 37
Ardfernal. Arg 2F 27
Ardfin. Arg 3E 27
Ardgartan. Arg 3D 39
Ardgay. High 4B 84
Ardgour. High 1B 46
Ardheslaig. High 4A 74
Ardindrean. High 1E 75
Ardlamont House. Arg 3D 29
Ardler. Per 3B 50
Ardlui. Arg 2E 39
Ardlussa. Arg 1A 28
Ardmair. High 4C 82
Ardmay. Arg 3D 39
Ardminish. Arg 1D 17
Ardmolich. High 4A 54
Ardmore. High 2D 87 (nr. Kinlochbervie)
Ardmore. High 1E 77 (nr. Tain)
Ardnacross. Arg 3C 44
Ardnadam. Arg 1F 29
Ardnagrask. High 1C 66
Ardnamurach. High 2B 54
Ardnarff. High 2B 64
Ardnastang. High 1F 45
Ardoch. Per 4F 49
Ardochy House. High 1F 55
Ardpatrick. Arg 3B 28
Ardrishaig. Arg 1C 28
Ardroag. High 1B 62
Ardross. High 2D 77
**Ardrossan.** N Ayr 1D 19
Ardshealach. High 1D 45
Ardslignish. High 1C 44
Ardtalla. Arg 4E 27
Ardtalnaig. Per 4C 48
Ardtoe. High 4F 53
Arduaine. Arg 2E 37
Ardullie. High 3C 76
Ardvasar. High 1F 53
Ardvorlich. Per 1B 40
Ardwell. Dum 3C 4
Ardwell. Mor 2E 69
Arean. High 4F 53
Aridhglas. Arg 1A 36
Arinacrinachd. High 4A 74
Arinagour. Arg 2H 91
Arisaig. High 3F 53
Ariundle. High 1F 45
Arivegaig. High 1D 45
Armadail. High 1F 53
Armadale. High 1F 53 (nr. Isleornsay)
Armadale. High 1C 88 (nr. Strathy)
Armadale. W Lot 3B 32
Armathwaite. Cumb 3E 9
Arncroach. Fife 3E 43
Arnicle. Arg 2E 17
Arnisdale. High 4B 64
Arnish. High 1E 63
Arniston. Midl 3F 33
Arnol. W Isl 2E 97
Arnprior. Stir 4B 40
Aros Mains. Arg 3C 44
Arpafeelie. High 4D 77
Arrochar. Arg 3D 39
Arscaig. High 2A 84
Artafallie. High 1D 67
Arthrath. Abers 2E 71
Arthurstone. Per 3B 50
Ascog. Arg 3F 29
Ashfield. Stir 3C 40
Ashgill. S Lan 1C 20
Ashgrove. Mor 3D 79
Ashkirk. Bord 3D 23
Ashton. Inv 2A 30
Askham. Cumb 4E 9
Aspatria. Cumb 3A 8
Astle. High 4C 84
Athelstaneford. E Lot 2B 34
Ath-Tharracail. High 1D 45
Attadale. High 2C 64
Aucharnie. Abers 1B 70
Auchattie. Abers 2B 60
Auchavan. Ang 1A 50
Auchbreck. Mor 3D 69
Auchenback. E Ren 4D 31
Auchenblae. Abers 4C 60
Auchenbrack. Dum 2C 12
Auchenbreck. Arg 1E 29
Auchencairn. Dum 2C 6 (nr. Dalbeattie)
Auchencairn. Dum 3E 13 (nr. Dumfries)
Auchencarroch. W Dun 1C 30
Auchencrow. Bord 3E 35
Auchendennan. Arg 1B 30
Auchendinny. Midl 3E 33
Auchengray. S Lan 4B 32
Auchenhalrig. Mor 3E 79
Auchenheath. S Lan 1D 21
Auchenlochan. Arg 2D 29
Auchenmade. N Ayr 1E 19
Auchenmalg. Dum 2D 5
Auchentiber. N Ayr 1E 19
Auchenvennel. Arg 1A 30
Auchindrain. Arg 3B 38
Auchininna. Abers 1B 70
Auchinleck. Dum 4F 11
Auchinleck. E Ayr 3A 20
Auchinloch. N Lan 2E 31
Auchinstarry. N Lan 2F 31
Auchleven. Abers 3B 70
Auchlochan. S Lan 2D 21
Auchlunachan. High 1E 75
Auchmillan. E Ayr 3A 20
Auchmithie. Ang 3F 51
Auchmuirbridge. Fife 3B 42
Auchmull. Ang 4A 60
Auchnacree. Ang 1D 51
Auchnafree. Per 4D 49
Auchnagallin. High 2B 68
Auchnagatt. Abers 1E 71
Aucholzie. Abers 2E 59
Auchreddie. Abers 1D 71
Auchterarder. Per 2E 41
Auchteraw. High 1A 56
Auchterderran. Fife 4B 42
Auchterhouse. Ang 4C 50
Auchtermuchty. Fife 2B 42
Auchterneed. High 4B 76
Auchtertool. Fife 4B 42
Auchtertyre. High 3B 64
Auchtubh. Stir 1A 40
Auckengill. High 1C 90
Auds. Abers 3B 80
Aughertree. Cumb 4B 8
Auldearn. High 4A 78
Auldgirth. Dum 3E 13
Auldhouse. S Lan 4E 31
Ault a' chruinn. High 3C 64
Aultbea. High 1B 74
Aultdearg. High 3F 75
Aultgrishan. High 1A 74
Aultguish Inn. High 2A 76
Aultibea. High 1F 85
Aultiphurst. High 1D 89
Aultivullin. High 1D 89
Aultmore. Mor 4F 79
Aultnamain Inn. High 1D 77
Avielochan. High 4A 68
**Aviemore.** High 102 (4F 67)

Avoch—Branderburgh


Avoch. *High* 4E 77
Avonbridge. *Falk* 2B 32
Ayle. *Nmbd* 3F 9
**Ayr.** *S Ayr* 103 (3E 19)
Ayres of Selivoe. *Shet* 2A 100
Ayton. *Bord* 3F 35
Aywick. *Shet* 3H 101

## B

Bac. *W Isl* 2F 97
Backaland. *Orkn* 4G 99
Backaskaill. *Orkn* 2F 99
Backfolds. *Abers* 4F 81
Backhill. *Abers* 2C 70
Backhill of Clackriach. *Abers* 1E 71
Backies. *High* 3D 85
Backmuir of New Gilston. *Fife* 3D 43
Back of Keppoch. *High* 3F 53
Badachonacher. *High* 2D 77
Badachro. *High* 2A 74
Badanloch Lodge. *High* 4C 88
Badavanich. *High* 4E 75
Badcall. *High* 2D 87
Badcaul. *High* 4B 82
Baddidarach. *High* 1B 82
Baddoch. *Abers* 3C 58
Badenscallie. *High* 3B 82
Badenscoth. *Abers* 2C 70
Badentarbat. *High* 2B 82
Badicaul. *High* 3A 64
Badlipster. *High* 3B 90
Badluarach. *High* 4A 82
Badnaban. *High* 1B 82
Badnabay. *High* 3D 87
Badnagie. *High* 4A 90
Badnellan. *High* 3D 85
Badninish. *High* 4C 84
Badrallach. *High* 4B 82
Bàgh a Chàise. *W Isl* 5D 94
Bàgh a' Chaisteil. *W Isl* 3B 92
Baghasdal. *W Isl* 1C 92
Bagh Mor. *W Isl* 2H 93
Bagh Shiarabhagh. *W Isl* 2C 92
Baile. *W Isl* 4D 94
Baile Ailein. *W Isl* 4D 96
Baile an Truiseil. *W Isl* 1E 97
Baile Boidheach. *Arg* 2B 28
Baile Glas. *W Isl* 2H 93
Bailemeonach. *Arg* 3D 45
Baile Mhanaich. *W Isl* 2G 93
Baile Mhartainn. *W Isl* 5B 94
Baile MhicPhail. *W Isl* 5C 94
Baile Mor. *W Isl* 1G 93
Baile Mór. *Arg* 5H 91
Baile nan Cailleach. *W Isl* 2G 93
Baile Raghaill. *W Isl* 1G 93
Baileyhead. *Cumb* 3E 15
Bailiesward. *Abers* 2F 69
Bail' Iochdrach. *W Isl* 2H 93
Baillieston. *Glas* 3E 31
Bail Uachdraich. *W Isl* 1H 93
Bail' Ur Tholastaidh. *W Isl* 2G 97
Bainsford. *Falk* 1A 32
Bainshole. *Abers* 2B 70
Baintown. *Fife* 3C 42
Balachuirn. *High* 1E 63
Balbeg. *High* 2B 66 (nr. Cannich)
Balbeg. *High* 3B 66 (nr. Loch Ness)
Balbeggie. *Per* 1A 42
Balblair. *High* 4A 84 (nr. Bonar Bridge)
Balblair. *High* 3E 77 (nr. Invergordon)
Balblair. *High* 1C 66 (nr. Inverness)
Balcathie. *Ang* 4F 51
Balchladich. *High* 4B 86
Balchraggan. *High* 1C 66
Balchrick. *High* 2C 86
Balcurvie. *Fife* 3C 42
Baldinnie. *Fife* 2D 43
Baldwinholme. *Cumb* 2C 8
Balearn. *Abers* 4F 81
Balemartine. *Arg* 3E 91
Balephetrish. *Arg* 3F 91
Balephuil. *Arg* 3E 91
Balerno. *Edin* 3D 33
Balevullin. *Arg* 3E 91
Balfield. *Ang* 1E 51
Balfour. *Orkn* 1C 98
Balfron. *Stir* 1D 31
Balgaveny. *Abers* 1B 70
Balgonar. *Fife* 4F 41
Balgowan. *High* 2D 57
Balgown. *High* 3C 72
Balgrochan. *E Dun* 2E 31
Balgy. *High* 4B 74
Balhalgardy. *Abers* 3C 70
Baliasta. *Shet* 1H 101
Baligill. *High* 1D 89
Balintore. *Ang* 2B 50
Balintore. *High* 2F 77
Balintraid. *High* 2E 77
Balkeerie. *Ang* 3C 50
Ballachulish. *High* 2B 46
Ballantrae. *S Ayr* 3B 10
Ballater. *Abers* 2E 59
Ballencrieff. *E Lot* 2A 34
Ballencrieff Toll. *W Lot* 2B 32
Ballentoul. *Per* 1D 49
Balliemore. *Arg* 1E 29 (nr. Dunoon)
Balliemore. *Arg* 1F 37 (nr. Oban)
Ballieward. *High* 2B 68
Ballimore. *Stir* 2A 40
Ballingry. *Fife* 4A 42
Ballinluig. *Per* 2E 49
Ballintuim. *Per* 2A 50
Balliveolan. *Arg* 3F 45
Balloan. *High* 3A 84
Balloch. *High* 1E 67
Balloch. *N Lan* 2F 31
Balloch. *Per* 2D 41
Balloch. *W Dun* 1B 30
Ballochan. *Abers* 2A 60
Ballochgoy. *Arg* 3E 29
Ballochmyle. *E Ayr* 3A 20
Ballochroy. *Arg* 4B 28
Ballygown. *Arg* 3B 44
Ballygrant. *Arg* 3D 27
Ballymichael. *N Ayr* 2A 18
Balmacara. *High* 3B 64
Balmaclellan. *Dum* 4B 12
Balmacqueen. *High* 2D 73
Balmaha. *Stir* 4F 39
Balmalcolm. *Fife* 3C 42
Balmalloch. *N Lan* 2F 31
Balmeanach. *High* 2E 63
Balmedie. *Abers* 4E 71
Balmerino. *Fife* 1C 42
Balmore. *E Dun* 2E 31
Balmore. *High* 1B 62
Balmullo. *Fife* 1D 43
Balmurrie. *Dum* 1D 5
Balnaboth. *Ang* 1C 50
Balnabruaich. *High* 2E 77
Balnabruich. *High* 1F 85
Balnacoil. *High* 2D 85
Balnacra. *High* 1C 64
Balnacroft. *Abers* 2D 59
Balnageith. *Mor* 4B 78
Balnaglaic. *High* 2B 66
Balnagrantach. *High* 2B 66
Balnaguard. *Per* 2E 49
Balnahard. *Arg* 4B 36
Balnain. *High* 2B 66
Balnakeil. *High* 1E 87
Balnaknock. *High* 3D 73
Balnamoon. *Abers* 4E 81
Balnamoon. *Ang* 1E 51
Balnapaling. *High* 3E 77
Balornock. *Glas* 3E 31
Balquhidder. *Stir* 1A 40
Baltasound. *Shet* 1H 101
Baltersan. *Dum* 1F 5
Balthangie. *Abers* 4D 81
Balvaird. *High* 4C 76
Balvaird. *Per* 2A 42
Balvenie. *Mor* 1E 69
Balvicar. *Arg* 2E 37
Balvraid. *High* 4B 64
Balvraid Lodge. *High* 2F 67
Bamburgh. *Nmbd* 2E 25
Banavie. *High* 4E 55
Banchory. *Abers* 2B 60
Banchory-Devenick. *Abers* 1E 61
Banff. *Abers* 3B 80
Bankend. *Dum* 1F 7
Bankfoot. *Per* 4F 49
Bankglen. *E Ayr* 4B 20
Bankhead. *Aber* 4D 71
Bankhead. *Abers* 1B 60
Bankhead. *S Lan* 1D 21
Banknock. *Falk* 2F 31
Banks. *Cumb* 1E 9
Bankshill. *Dum* 3A 14
Banniskirk. *High* 2A 90
Bannockburn. *Stir* 4D 41
Banton. *N Lan* 2F 31
Barabhas. *W Isl* 1E 97
Barabhas Iarach. *W Isl* 2E 97
Baramore. *High* 4F 53
Barassie. *S Ayr* 2E 19
Baravullin. *Arg* 3A 46
Barbaraville. *High* 2E 77
Barbhas Uarach. *W Isl* 1E 97
Barbieston. *S Ayr* 4F 19
Barcaldine. *Arg* 3A 46
Barclose. *Cumb* 1D 9
Bardister. *Shet* 4F 101
Bardnabeinne. *High* 4C 84
Bardowie. *E Dun* 2D 31
Bardrainney. *Inv* 2B 30
Barelees. *Nmbd* 2B 24
Bargeddie. *N Lan* 3E 31
Bargrennan. *Dum* 4E 11
Barharrow. *Dum* 2B 6
Barlanark. *Glas* 3E 31
Barmoor. *Nmbd* 2D 25
Barmulloch. *Glas* 3E 31
Barnbarroch. *Dum* 2D 7
Barnhead. *Ang* 2F 51
Barnhill. *D'dee* 4D 51
Barnhill. *Mor* 4C 78
Barnhill. *Per* 1A 42
Barnhills. *Dum* 4A 10
Barony, The. *Orkn* 1A 98
Barr. *Dum* 1C 12
Barr. *S Ayr* 2D 11
Barra Airport. *W Isl* 2B 92
Barrachan. *Dum* 3E 5
Barraglom. *W Isl* 3C 96
Barrahormid. *Arg* 1B 28
Barrapol. *Arg* 3E 91
Barravullin. *Arg* 3F 37
**Barrhead.** *E Ren* 4D 31
Barrhill. *S Ayr* 3D 11
Barrmill. *N Ayr* 4B 30
Barrock. *High* 5A 98
Barrowburn. *Nmbd* 4B 24
Barry. *Ang* 4E 51
Barthol Chapel. *Abers* 2D 71
Barton. *Cumb* 4D 9
Bassendean. *Bord* 1F 23
Bassenthwaite. *Cumb* 4B 8
Basta. *Shet* 2H 101
**Bathgate.** *W Lot* 3B 32
Bathville. *W Lot* 3B 32
Bauds of Cullen. *Mor* 3F 79
Baugh. *Arg* 3F 91
Bay. *High* 4B 72
Beacrabhaic. *W Isl* 3F 95
Beadnell. *Nmbd* 3F 25
Beal. *Nmbd* 1D 25
Beanley. *Nmbd* 4D 25
Beaquoy. *Orkn* 5E 99
**Bearsden.** *E Dun* 2D 31
Beattock. *Dum* 1F 13
Beauly. *High* 1C 66
Beaumont. *Cumb* 2C 8
Beckfoot. *Cumb* 3F 7
Bedrule. *Bord* 4F 23
Beeswing. *Dum* 1D 7
Beinn Casgro. *W Isl* 4F 97
Beith. *N Ayr* 4B 30
Belfatton. *Abers* 4F 81
Belford. *Nmbd* 2E 25
Belhaven. *E Lot* 2C 34
Belhelvie. *Abers* 4E 71
Belhinnie. *Abers* 3F 69
Bellabeg. *Abers* 4E 69
Belladrum. *High* 1C 66
Bellamore. *S Ayr* 3D 11
Bellanoch. *Arg* 4F 37
Belleheiglash. *Mor* 2C 68
Belle Vue. *Cumb* 4A 8
Bellfield. *S Lan* 2D 21
Belliehill. *Ang* 1E 51
Bellochantuy. *Arg* 2D 17
Bellsbank. *E Ayr* 1F 11
**Bellshill.** *N Lan* 4F 31
Bellshill. *Nmbd* 2E 25
Bellside. *N Lan* 4A 32
Bellspool. *Bord* 2A 22
Bellsquarry. *W Lot* 3C 32
Belmaduthy. *High* 4D 77
Belmont. *Shet* 1H 101
Belmont. *S Ayr* 3E 19
Belnacraig. *Abers* 4E 69
Belston. *S Ayr* 3E 19
Belts of Collonach. *Abers* 2B 60
Bemersyde. *Bord* 2E 23
Ben Alder Lodge. *High* 4C 56
Ben Armine Lodge. *High* 2C 84
Benbecula Airport. *W Isl* 2G 93
Benbuie. *Dum* 2C 12
Benderloch. *Arg* 4A 46
Bendronaig Lodge. *High* 2D 65
Benholm. *Abers* 4D 61
Benmore Lodge. *High* 2E 83
Bennecarrigan. *N Ayr* 3A 18
Bennethead. *Cumb* 4D 9
Benston. *Shet* 1C 100
Benstonhall. *Orkn* 4G 99
Bent. *Abers* 4B 60
Bentpath. *Dum* 2C 14
Bents. *W Lot* 3B 32
Benvie. *D'dee* 4C 50
Beoraidbeg. *High* 2F 53
Bernera. *High* 3B 64
Bernice. *Arg* 4C 38
Bernisdale. *High* 4D 73
Berriedale. *High* 1F 85
Berrier. *Cumb* 4C 8
Berrington. *Nmbd* 1D 25
Berrington Law. *Nmbd* 1C 24
Berryhillock. *Mor* 3A 80
Berryscaur. *Dum* 2A 14
**Berwick-upon-Tweed.** *Nmbd* 4F 35
Bettyhill. *High* 1C 88
Beul an Atha. *Arg* 3D 27
Bewaldeth. *Cumb* 4B 8
Bewcastle. *Cumb* 4E 15
Bhalton. *W Isl* 3B 96
Bhatarsaigh. *W Isl* 3B 92
Biddlestone. *Nmbd* 4C 24
Bieldside. *Aber* 1D 61
Biggar. *S Lan* 2F 21
Bighouse. *High* 1D 89
Biglands. *Cumb* 2B 8
Big Sand. *High* 2A 74
Bigton. *Shet* 4B 100
Bilbster. *High* 2B 90
Bilston. *Midl* 3E 33
Bilton. *Nmbd* 4F 25
Bimbister. *Orkn* 1B 98
Bindal. *High* 1A 78
Binniehill. *Falk* 2A 32
Birchburn. *N Ayr* 3A 18
Birchview. *Mor* 2C 68
Birdston. *E Dun* 2E 31
Birgham. *Bord* 2A 24
Birichen. *High* 4C 84
Birkby. *Cumb* 4F 7
Birkenhills. *Abers* 1C 70
Birkenshaw. *N Lan* 3E 31
Birkhall. *Abers* 2E 59
Birkhill. *Ang* 4C 50
Birling. *Nmbd* 4F 25
Birnam. *Per* 3F 49
Birse. *Abers* 2A 60
Birsemore. *Abers* 2A 60
**Bishopbriggs.** *E Dun* 2E 31
Bishopmill. *Mor* 3D 79
Bishopton. *Dum* 3F 5
Bishopton. *Ren* 2C 30
Bixter. *Shet* 1B 100
Blackburn. *Abers* 4D 71
Blackburn. *W Lot* 3B 32
Black Clauchrie. *S Ayr* 3D 11
Black Corries. *High* 2D 47
Black Crofts. *Arg* 4A 46
Blackdog. *Abers* 4E 71
Blackdyke. *Cumb* 2A 8
Blackford. *Cumb* 1C 8
Blackford. *Per* 3D 41
Blackhall. *Edin* 2D 33
Blackhall. *Ren* 3C 30
Blackhill. *Abers* 1F 71
Blackhill. *High* 4C 72
Blackhills. *Abers* 3E 81
Blackhills. *High* 4A 78
Blacklunans. *Per* 1A 50
Black Mount. *Arg* 3D 47
Blackness. *Falk* 2C 32
Blackpool Gate. *Cumb* 4E 15
Blackridge. *W Lot* 3A 32
Blackrock. *Arg* 3D 27
Blackshaw. *Dum* 1F 7
Blacktop. *Aber* 1D 61
Blackwaterfoot. *N Ayr* 3F 17
Blackwood. *Dum* 3E 13
Blackwood. *S Lan* 1C 20
Bladnoch. *Dum* 2F 5
Blagill. *Cumb* 3F 9
Blaich. *High* 4D 55
Blain. *High* 1D 45
Blair Atholl. *Per* 1D 49
Blair Drummond. *Stir* 4C 40
Blairgowrie. *Per* 3A 50
Blairhall. *Fife* 1C 32
Blairingone. *Per* 4E 41
Blairlogie. *Stir* 4D 41
Blairmore. *Abers* 2F 69
Blairmore. *Arg* 1F 29
Blairmore. *High* 2C 86
Blairquhanan. *W Dun* 1C 30
Blandy. *High* 1B 88
Blanefield. *Stir* 2D 31
**Blantyre.** *S Lan* 4E 31
Blarmachfoldach. *High* 1B 46
Blarnalearoch. *High* 4C 82
Blathaisbhal. *W Isl* 5C 94
Blebocraigs. *Fife* 2D 43
Blencarn. *Cumb* 4F 9
Blencogo. *Cumb* 3A 8
Blennerhasset. *Cumb* 3A 8
Blindburn. *Nmbd* 4B 24
Blindcrake. *Cumb* 4A 8
Blitterlees. *Cumb* 2A 8
Bloomfield. *Bord* 3E 23
Blyth. *Bord* 1A 22
Blyth Bank. *Bord* 1A 22
Blyth Bridge. *Bord* 1A 22
Boarhills. *Fife* 2E 43
Boath. *High* 2C 76
Boat of Garten. *High* 4A 68
Boddam. *Abers* 1F 71
Boddam. *Shet* 5B 100
Bogallan. *High* 4D 77
Bogbrae Croft. *Abers* 2F 71
Bogend. *S Ayr* 2E 19
Boghall. *Midl* 3E 33
Boghall. *W Lot* 3B 32
Boghead. *S Lan* 1C 20
Bogindollo. *Ang* 2D 51
Bogmoor. *Mor* 3E 79
Bogniebrae. *Abers* 1A 70
Bograxie. *Abers* 4C 70
Bogside. *N Lan* 4A 32
Bogton. *Abers* 4B 80
Bogue. *Dum* 3B 12
Bohenie. *High* 3F 55
Boirseam. *W Isl* 4E 95
Boleside. *Bord* 2D 23
Bolshan. *Ang* 2F 51
Boltachan. *Per* 2D 49
Bolton. *E Lot* 2B 34
Bolton. *Nmbd* 4E 25
Boltonfellend. *Cumb* 1D 9
Boltongate. *Cumb* 3B 8
Bolton Low Houses. *Cumb* 3B 8
Bolton New Houses. *Cumb* 3B 8
Bolton Wood Lane. *Cumb* 3B 8
Bonar Bridge. *High* 4B 84
Bonawe. *Arg* 4B 46
Bonchester Bridge. *Bord* 4E 23
**Bo'ness.** *Falk* 1B 32
**Bonhill.** *W Dun* 2B 30
Bonjedward. *Bord* 3F 23
Bonkle. *N Lan* 4A 32
Bonnington. *Ang* 4E 51
Bonnington. *Edin* 3D 33
Bonnybank. *Fife* 3C 42
**Bonnybridge.** *Falk* 1A 32
Bonnykelly. *Abers* 4D 81
**Bonnyrigg.** *Midl* 3F 33
Bonnyton. *Ang* 4C 50
Bonnytown. *Fife* 2E 43
Booth of Toft. *Shet* 4G 101
Boquhan. *Stir* 1D 31
Bordlands. *Bord* 1A 22
Boreland. *Dum* 2A 14
Borestone Brae. *Stir* 4C 40
Borgh. *W Isl* 2B 92 (on Barra)
Borgh. *W Isl* 2G 93 (on Benbecula)
Borgh. *W Isl* 4D 94 (on Berneray)
Borgh. *W Isl* 1F 97 (on Isle of Lewis)
Borghasdal. *W Isl* 4E 95
Borghastan. *W Isl* 2C 96
Borgh na Sgiotaig. *High* 2C 72
Borgie. *High* 2B 88
Borgue. *Dum* 3B 6
Borgue. *High* 1F 85
Borlum. *High* 3C 66
Bornais. *W Isl* 5G 93
Bornesketaig. *High* 2C 72
Borreraig. *High* 4A 72
Borrobol Lodge. *High* 1D 85
Borrodale. *High* 1A 62
Borrowston. *High* 3C 90
Borrowstonehill. *Orkn* 2C 98
Borrowstoun. *Falk* 1B 32
Borthwick. *Midl* 4F 33
Borve. *High* 1D 63
Bostadh. *W Isl* 2C 96
Bothel. *Cumb* 4A 8
Bothwell. *S Lan* 4F 31
Bottacks. *High* 3B 76
Bottomcraig. *Fife* 1C 42
Boulmer. *Nmbd* 4F 25
Bousd. *Arg* 1H 91
Bousta. *Shet* 1A 100
Boustead Hill. *Cumb* 2B 8
Bowden. *Bord* 2E 23
Bower. *Nmbd* 3F 15
Bowermadden. *High* 1B 90
Bowershall. *Fife* 4F 41
Bowertower. *High* 1B 90
Bowhousebog. *N Lan* 4A 32
Bowling. *W Dun* 2C 30
Bowmore. *Arg* 4D 27
Bowness-on-Solway. *Cumb* 1B 8
Bow of Fife. *Fife* 2C 42
Bowriefauld. *Ang* 3E 51
Bowscale. *Cumb* 4C 8
Bowsden. *Nmbd* 1C 24
Bowside Lodge. *High* 1D 89
Boyndie. *Abers* 3B 80
Braal Castle. *High* 2A 90
Brabster. *High* 1C 90
Bracadale. *High* 2C 62
Bracara. *High* 2A 54
Brackenlands. *Cumb* 3B 8
Brackenthwaite. *Cumb* 3B 8
Brackla. *High* 4F 77
Brackletter. *High* 3E 55
Brackloch. *High* 1C 82
Braco. *Per* 3D 41
Bracobrae. *Mor* 4A 80
Bradford. *Nmbd* 2E 25
Brae. *High* 1B 74
Brae. *Shet* 5F 101
Braeantra. *High* 2C 76
Braefield. *High* 2B 66
Braefindon. *High* 4D 77
Braegrum. *Per* 1F 41
Braehead. *Ang* 2F 51
Braehead. *Dum* 2F 5
Braehead. *Mor* 1D 69
Braehead. *Orkn* 3F 99
Braehead. *S Lan* 2D 21 (nr. Coalburn)
Braehead. *S Lan* 4B 32 (nr. Forth)
Braehoulland. *Shet* 4E 101
Braemar. *Abers* 2C 58
Braemore. *High* 4F 89 (nr. Dunbeath)
Braemore. *High* 2E 75 (nr. Ullapool)
Brae of Achnahaird. *High* 2B 82
Brae Roy Lodge. *High* 2A 56
Braeside. *Abers* 2E 71
Braeside. *Inv* 2A 30
Braes of Coul. *Ang* 2B 50
Braeswick. *Orkn* 4H 99
Braetongue. *High* 2A 88
Braeval. *Stir* 3A 40
Braevallich. *Arg* 3A 38
Braewick. *Shet* 1B 100
Bragar. *W Isl* 2D 96
Bragleenbeg. *Arg* 1A 38
Braidwood. *S Lan* 1D 21
Braigo. *Arg* 3C 26
Braithwaite. *Cumb* 4B 8
Brampton. *Cumb* 1E 9
Branault. *High* 1C 44
Branchill. *Mor* 4B 78
Branderburgh. *Mor* 2D 79

Clachan—Dalsmirren


Clachan. *Arg* 4B **28**
(on Kintyre)
Clachan. *Arg* 3F **45**
(on Lismore)
Clachan. *High* 1C **88**
(nr. Bettyhill)
Clachan. *High* 3D **73**
(nr. Staffin)
Clachan. *High* 2D **73**
(nr. Uig)
Clachan. *High* 2E **63**
(on Raasay)
Clachan Farm. *Arg* 2C **38**
Clachan na Luib. *W Isl* 1H **93**
Clachan of Campsie. *E Dun* 2E **31**
Clachan of Glendaruel. *Arg* 1D **29**
Clachan-Seil. *Arg* 2E **37**
Clachan Shannda. *W Isl* 5C **94**
Clachan Strachur. *Arg* 3B **38**
Clachbreck. *Arg* 2B **28**
Clachnaharry. *High* 1D **67**
Clachtoll. *High* 1B **82**
Clackmannan. *Clac* 4E **41**
**Clackmannanshire Bridge**. *Clac* 1B **32**
Clackmarras. *Mor* 4D **79**
Cladach a Chaolais. *W Isl* 1G **93**
Cladach Chairinis. *W Isl* 2H **93**
Cladach Chirceboist. *W Isl* 1G **93**
Cladach Iolaraigh. *W Isl* 1G **93**
Cladich. *Arg* 1B **38**
Claggan. *High* 4E **55**
(nr. Fort William)
Claggan. *High* 2E **45**
(nr. Lochaline)
Claigan. *High* 4B **72**
Claonaig. *Arg* 4C **28**
Clappers. *Bord* 4F **35**
Clapphoull. *Shet* 4C **100**
Clarebrand. *Dum* 1C **6**
Clarencefield. *Dum* 1F **7**
Clarilaw. *Bord* 4E **23**
**Clarkston**. *E Ren* 4D **31**
Clasheddy. *High* 1B **88**
Clashindarroch. *Abers* 2F **69**
Clashmore. *High* 1E **77**
(nr. Dornoch)
Clashmore. *High* 4B **86**
(nr. Stoer)
Clashnessie. *High* 4B **86**
Clashnoir. *Mor* 3D **69**
Clate. *Shet* 5H **101**
Clathick. *Per* 1D **41**
Clathy. *Per* 2E **41**
Clatt. *Abers* 3A **70**
Claygate. *Dum* 4C **14**
Clayholes. *Ang* 4E **51**
Clayock. *High* 2A **90**
Cleadale. *High* 3D **53**
Cleat. *Orkn* 3F **99**
(nr. Braehead)
Cleat. *Orkn* 4C **98**
(nr. St Margaret's Hope)
Cleekhimin. *N Lan* 4F **31**
Cleigh. *Arg* 1F **37**
Cleish. *Per* 4F **41**
Cleland. *N Lan* 4A **32**
Clennell. *Nmbd* 4C **24**
Clephanton. *High* 4F **77**
Clerkhill. *High* 1C **88**
Clestrain. *Orkn* 2B **98**
Cliaid. *W Isl* 2B **92**
Cliasmol. *W Isl* 2E **95**
Clibberswick. *Shet* 1H **101**
Cliburn. *Cumb* 4E **9**
Cliffburn. *Ang* 3F **51**
Clifton. *Cumb* 4E **9**
Clifton. *Stir* 4E **47**
Climpy. *S Lan* 4B **32**
Clintmains. *Bord* 2F **23**
Cliobh. *W Isl* 3B **96**
Cliuthar. *W Isl* 3F **95**
Clivocast. *Shet* 1H **101**
Clochan. *Mor* 3F **79**
Clochforbie. *Abers* 4D **81**
Cloddymoss. *Mor* 3A **78**
Clola. *Abers* 1F **71**
Closeburn. *Dum* 2D **13**
Clousta. *Shet* 1B **100**
Clouston. *Orkn* 1A **98**
Clova. *Abers* 3F **69**
Clova. *Ang* 4E **59**
Clovenfords. *Bord* 2D **23**
Clovenstone. *Abers* 4C **70**
Clovullin. *High* 1B **46**
Cluanie Inn. *High* 4D **65**
Cluanie Lodge. *High* 4D **65**
Clunas. *High* 1F **67**
Clune. *High* 3E **67**
Clunes. *High* 3F **55**
Clunie. *Per* 3A **50**
Cluny. *Fife* 4B **42**
**Clydebank**. *W Dun* 3D **31**
Clynder. *Arg* 1A **30**
Clynelish. *High* 3D **85**
Clyth. *High* 4B **90**
Cnip. *W Isl* 3B **96**
Cnoc Amhlaigh. *W Isl* 3G **97**
Coalburn. *S Lan* 2D **21**
Coalford. *Abers* 2D **61**
Coalhall. *E Ayr* 4F **19**
Coalsnaughton. *Clac* 4E **41**
Coaltown of Balgonie. *Fife* 4C **42**
Coaltown of Wemyss. *Fife* 4C **42**
Coanwood. *Nmbd* 2F **9**
**Coatbridge**. *N Lan* 3F **31**
Coatdyke. *N Lan* 3F **31**
Cock Bridge. *Abers* 1D **59**
Cockburnspath. *Bord* 2D **35**
Cockenzie and Port Seton. *E Lot* 2A **34**
Cockermouth. *Cumb* 4A **8**
Cocklaw. *Abers* 1F **71**
Cockmuir. *Abers* 4E **81**
Coignafearn Lodge. *High* 4D **67**
Coig Peighinnean. *W Isl* 1G **97**
Coig Peighinnean Bhuirgh. *W Isl* 1F **97**
Coilleag. *W Isl* 1C **92**
Coillemore. *High* 2D **77**
Coillore. *High* 2C **62**
Coire an Fhuarain. *W Isl* 3D **96**
Col. *W Isl* 2F **97**
Colaboll. *High* 2A **84**
Colbost. *High* 1B **62**
Coldbackie. *High* 2B **88**
Coldingham. *Bord* 3F **35**
Coldrain. *Per* 3F **41**
Coldstream. *Bord* 1B **24**
Coldwells. *Abers* 2F **71**
Coldwells Croft. *Abers* 3A **70**
Cole. *Shet* 5F **101**
Coleburn. *Mor* 4D **79**
Colinsburgh. *Fife* 3D **43**
Colinton. *Edin* 3E **33**
Colintraive. *Arg* 2E **29**
Collace. *Per* 4B **50**
Collam. *W Isl* 3F **95**
College of Roseisle. *Mor* 3C **78**
Collessie. *Fife* 2B **42**
Collieston. *Abers* 3F **71**
Collin. *Dum* 4F **13**
Colliston. *Ang* 3F **51**
Collydean. *Fife* 3B **42**
Colmonell. *S Ayr* 3C **10**
Colpy. *Abers* 2B **70**
Colstoun House. *E Lot* 2B **34**
Coltfield. *Mor* 3C **78**
Coltness. *N Lan* 4A **32**
Col Uarach. *W Isl* 3F **97**
Colvend. *Dum* 2D **7**
Colvister. *Shet* 2H **101**
Comers. *Abers* 1B **60**
Comrie. *Fife* 1C **32**
Comrie. *Per* 1C **40**
Conaglen. *High* 1B **46**
Conchra. *Arg* 1E **29**
Conchra. *High* 3B **64**
Condorrat. *N Lan* 2F **31**
Conicaval. *Mor* 4A **78**
Conisby. *Arg* 3C **26**
Connel. *Arg* 4A **46**
Connel Park. *E Ayr* 4B **20**
Connista. *High* 2D **73**
Conon Bridge. *High* 4C **76**
Cononsyth. *Ang* 3E **51**
Conordan. *High* 2E **63**
Contin. *High* 4B **76**
Contullich. *High* 2D **77**
Cookney. *Abers* 2D **61**
Copister. *Shet* 4G **101**
Copshaw Holm. *Bord* 3D **15**
Cordon. *N Ayr* 2B **18**
Corgarff. *Abers* 1D **59**
Corlae. *Dum* 2B **12**
Cormiston. *S Lan* 2F **21**
Cornaigbeg. *Arg* 3E **91**
Cornaigmore. *Arg* 1H **91**
(on Coll)
Cornaigmore. *Arg* 3E **91**
(on Tiree)
Cornhill. *Abers* 4A **80**
Cornhill. *High* 4A **84**
Cornhill-on-Tweed. *Nmbd* 2B **24**
Cornquoy. *Orkn* 2D **98**
Corntown. *High* 4C **76**
Corpach. *High* 4D **55**
Corra. *Dum* 1D **7**
Corran. *High* 1B **46**
(nr. Arnisdale)
Corran. *High* 1B **54**
(nr. Fort William)
Corribeg. *High* 4C **54**
Corrie. *N Ayr* 1B **18**
Corrie Common. *Dum* 3B **14**
Corriecravie. *N Ayr* 3A **18**
Corriekinloch. *High* 1E **83**
Corriemoillie. *High* 3A **76**
Corrievarkie Lodge. *Per* 4C **56**
Corrievorrie. *High* 3E **67**
Corrigall. *Orkn* 1B **98**
Corrimony. *High* 2A **66**
Corrour Shooting Lodge. *High* 1F **47**
Corry. *High* 3F **63**
Corrybrough. *High* 3F **67**
Corrygills. *N Ayr* 2B **18**
Corry of Ardnagrask. *High* 1C **66**
Corsback. *High* 5A **98**
(nr. Dunnet)
Corsback. *High* 2B **90**
(nr. Halkirk)
Corse. *Abers* 1B **70**
Corsehill. *Abers* 4E **81**
Corse of Kinnoir. *Abers* 1A **70**
Corsock. *Dum* 4C **12**
Corstorphine. *Edin* 2E **33**
Cortachy. *Ang* 2C **50**
Corwar House. *S Ayr* 3D **11**
Costa. *Orkn* 5E **99**
Cotehill. *Cumb* 2D **9**
Cothal. *Abers* 4D **71**
Cott. *Orkn* 5H **99**
Cottartown. *High* 2B **68**
Cottown. *Abers* 1D **71**
Coulags. *High* 1C **64**
Coulin Lodge. *High* 4D **75**
Coull. *Abers* 1A **60**
Coulport. *Arg* 1A **30**
Coulter. *S Lan* 2F **21**
Coupar Angus. *Per* 3B **50**
Coupland. *Nmbd* 2C **24**
Cour. *Arg* 1F **17**
Courance. *Dum* 2F **13**
Courteachan. *High* 2F **53**
Cousland. *Midl* 3F **33**
Coustonn. *Arg* 2E **29**
Cove. *Arg* 1A **30**
Cove. *High* 1B **74**
Cove. *Bord* 2D **35**
Cove Bay. *Aber* 1E **61**
Covesea. *Mor* 2C **78**
Covington. *S Lan* 2E **21**
**Cowdenbeath**. *Fife* 4A **42**
Cowdenburn. *Bord* 4E **33**
Cowdenend. *Fife* 4A **42**
Cowfords. *Mor* 3E **79**
Cowie. *Abers* 3D **61**
Cowie. *Stir* 1A **32**
Cowstrandburn. *Fife* 4F **41**
Coylton. *S Ayr* 4F **19**
Coylumbridge. *High* 4A **68**
Coynach. *Abers* 1F **59**
Coynachie. *Abers* 2F **69**
Crackaig. *High* 2E **85**
Cradhlastadh. *W Isl* 3B **96**
Cragabus. *Arg* 1A **16**
Craggan. *High* 3B **68**
Cragganmore. *Mor* 2C **68**
Cragganvallie. *High* 2C **66**
Craggie. *High* 2D **85**
Craggiemore. *High* 2E **67**
Craichie. *Ang* 3E **51**
Craig. *Arg* 4B **46**
Craig. *Dum* 4B **12**
Craig. *High* 1D **65**
(nr. Achnashellach)
Craig. *High* 3A **74**
(nr. Lower Diabaig)
Craig. *High* 2B **64**
(nr. Stromeferry)
Craiganour Lodge. *Per* 2B **48**
Craigbrack. *Arg* 4C **38**
Craigdallie. *Per* 1B **42**
Craigdam. *Abers* 2D **71**
Craigdarroch. *E Ayr* 1B **12**
Craigdarroch. *High* 4B **76**
Craigdhu. *High* 1B **66**
Craigearn. *Abers* 4C **70**
Craigellachie. *Mor* 1D **69**
Craigend. *Per* 1A **42**
Craigendoran. *Arg* 1B **30**
Craigends. *Ren* 3C **30**
Craigenputtock. *Dum* 3C **12**
Craigens. *E Ayr* 4A **20**
Craighall. *Edin* 2D **33**
Craighead. *Fife* 2F **43**
Craighouse. *Arg* 3F **27**
Craigie. *Abers* 4E **71**
Craigie. *D'dee* 4D **51**
Craigie. *Per* 3A **50**
(nr. Blairgowrie)
Craigie. *Per* 1A **42**
(nr. Perth)
Craigie. *S Ayr* 2F **19**
Craigielaw. *E Lot* 2A **34**
Craiglemine. *Dum* 4F **5**
Craiglockhart. *Edin* 2E **33**
Craig Lodge. *Arg* 2E **29**
Craigmalloch. *E Ayr* 2F **11**
Craigmaud. *Abers* 4D **81**
Craigmill. *Stir* 4D **41**
Craigmillar. *Edin* 2E **33**
Craigmore. *Arg* 3F **29**
Craigmuie. *Dum* 3C **12**
Craignair. *Dum* 1D **7**
Craigneuk. *N Lan* 3F **31**
(nr. Airdrie)
Craigneuk. *N Lan* 4F **31**
(nr. Motherwell)
Craignure. *Arg* 4E **45**
Craigo. *Ang* 1F **51**
Craigrory. *High* 1D **67**
Craigrothie. *Fife* 2C **42**
Craigs. *Dum* 4B **14**
Craigs, The. *High* 4F **83**
Craigshill. *W Lot* 3C **32**
Craigton. *Aber* 1D **61**
Craigton. *Abers* 4C **70**
Craigton. *Ang* 4E **51**
(nr. Carnoustie)
Craigton. *Ang* 2C **50**
(nr. Kirriemuir)
Craigton. *High* 1D **67**
Craigtown. *High* 2D **89**
Craik. *Bord* 1C **14**
Crail. *Fife* 3F **43**
Crailing. *Bord* 3F **23**
Crailinghall. *Bord* 3F **23**
Cramond. *Edin* 2D **33**
Cramond Bridge. *Edin* 2D **33**
Cranloch. *Mor* 4D **79**
Crannich. *Arg* 3C **44**
Crannoch. *Mor* 4F **79**
Cranshaws. *Bord* 3C **34**
Craobh Haven. *Arg* 3E **37**
Craobhnaclag. *High* 1B **66**
Crarae. *Arg* 4A **38**
Crask. *High* 1C **88**
(nr. Bettyhill)
Crask. *High* 1A **84**
(nr. Lairg)
Crask of Aigas. *High* 1B **66**
Craster. *Nmbd* 3F **25**
Crathes. *Abers* 2C **60**
Crathie. *Abers* 2D **59**
Crathie. *High* 2C **56**
Crawford. *S Lan* 3E **21**
Crawforddyke. *S Lan* 4A **32**
Crawfordjohn. *S Lan* 3D **21**
Crawick. *Dum* 4C **20**
Crawton. *Abers* 3D **61**
Cray. *Per* 1A **50**
Creagan. *Arg* 3A **46**
Creag Aoil. *High* 4E **55**
Creag Ghoraidh. *W Isl* 3G **93**
Creaguaineach Lodge. *High* 1E **47**
Creca. *Dum* 4B **14**
Creebridge. *Dum* 1F **5**
Creetown. *Dum* 2F **5**
Creggans. *Arg* 3B **38**
Creich. *Arg* 1A **36**
Creich. *Fife* 1C **42**
Crepkill. *High* 1D **63**
**Crianlarich**. *Stir* 1E **39**
Crichton. *Midl* 3F **33**
Crieff. *Per* 1D **41**
Crimond. *Abers* 4F **81**
Crimonmogate. *Abers* 4F **81**
Crinan. *Arg* 4E **37**
Crocketford. *Dum* 4D **13**
Croftamie. *Stir* 1C **30**
Croftfoot. *Glas* 3D **31**
Croftmill. *Per* 4D **49**
Crofton. *Cumb* 2C **8**
Crofts. *Dum* 4C **12**
Crofts of Benachielt. *High* 4A **90**
Crofts of Dipple. *Mor* 4E **79**
Croggan. *Arg* 1E **37**
Croglin. *Cumb* 3E **9**
Croich. *High* 4F **83**
Croick. *High* 2D **89**
Croig. *Arg* 2A **44**
Cromarty. *High* 3E **77**
Crombie. *Fife* 1C **32**
Cromdale. *High* 3B **68**
Cromor. *W Isl* 4F **97**
Cromra. *High* 3C **56**
Cronberry. *E Ayr* 3B **20**
Crookdake. *Cumb* 3A **8**
Crookedholm. *E Ayr* 2F **19**
Crookham. *Nmbd* 2C **24**
Crook of Devon. *Per* 3F **41**
Crookston. *Glas* 3D **31**
Cros. *W Isl* 1G **97**
Crosbie. *N Ayr* 4A **30**
Crosbost. *W Isl* 4E **97**
Crosby. *Cumb* 4F **7**
Crosby Villa. *Cumb* 4F **7**
Crossaig. *Arg* 4C **28**
Crossapol. *Arg* 3E **91**
Crosscanonby. *Cumb* 4F **7**
Crossford. *Fife* 1C **32**
Crossford. *S Lan* 1D **21**
Crossgate. *Orkn* 1C **98**
Crossgatehall. *E Lot* 3F **33**
Crossgates. *Fife* 1D **33**
Crosshands. *E Ayr* 2F **19**
Crosshill. *E Ayr* 3F **19**
Crosshill. *Fife* 4A **42**
Crosshill. *S Ayr* 1E **11**
Crosshills. *High* 2D **77**
Crosshouse. *E Ayr* 2E **19**
Crossings. *Cumb* 4E **15**
Crosskirk. *High* 1F **89**
Crosslee. *Ren* 3C **30**
Crossmichael. *Dum* 1C **6**
Cross of Jackston. *Abers* 2C **70**
Crossroads. *Abers* 1E **61**
(nr. Aberdeen)
Crossroads. *Abers* 2C **60**
(nr. Banchory)
Crossroads. *E Ayr* 2F **19**
Crosston. *Ang* 2E **51**
Crothair. *W Isl* 3C **96**
Crovie. *Abers* 3D **81**
Croy. *High* 1E **67**
Croy. *N Lan* 2F **31**
Crubenbeg. *High* 2D **57**
Crubenmore Lodge. *High* 2D **57**
Cruden Bay. *Abers* 2F **71**
Crudie. *Abers* 4C **80**
Crulabhig. *W Isl* 3C **96**
Cuaich. *High* 3D **57**
Cuaig. *High* 4A **74**
Cuan. *Arg* 2E **37**
Cuckron. *Shet* 1C **100**
Cuidhir. *W Isl* 2B **92**
Cuidhsiadar. *W Isl* 1G **97**
Cuidhtinis. *W Isl* 4E **95**
Culbo. *High* 3D **77**
Culbokie. *High* 4D **77**
Culburnie. *High* 1B **66**
Culcabock. *High* 1D **67**
Culcharry. *High* 4F **77**
Culduie. *High* 1A **64**
Culeave. *High* 4A **84**
Culgaith. *Cumb* 4F **9**
Culkein. *High* 4B **86**
Culkein Drumbeg. *High* 4C **86**
Cullen. *Mor* 3A **80**
Cullicudden. *High* 3D **77**
Cullipool. *Arg* 2E **37**
Cullivoe. *Shet* 1H **101**
Culloch. *Per* 2C **40**
Culloden. *High* 1E **67**
Cul na Caepaich. *High* 3F **53**
Culnacnoc. *High* 3E **73**
Culnacraig. *High* 3B **82**
Culrain. *High* 4A **84**
Culross. *Fife* 1B **32**
Culroy. *S Ayr* 4E **19**
Culswick. *Shet* 2A **100**
Cults. *Aber* 1D **61**
Cults. *Abers* 2A **70**
Cults. *Fife* 3C **42**
Cultybraggan Camp. *Per* 1C **40**
Culzie Lodge. *High* 2C **76**
**Cumbernauld**. *N Lan* 2F **31**
Cumbernauld Village. *N Lan* 2F **31**
Cumdivock. *Cumb* 3C **8**
Cuminestown. *Abers* 4D **81**
Cumledge Mill. *Bord* 4D **35**
Cumlewick. *Shet* 4C **100**
Cummersdale. *Cumb* 2C **8**
Cummertrees. *Dum* 1A **8**
Cummingstown. *Mor* 3C **78**
Cumnock. *E Ayr* 3A **20**
Cumrew. *Cumb* 2E **9**
Cumwhinton. *Cumb* 2D **9**
Cumwhitton. *Cumb* 2E **9**
Cunninghamhead. *N Ayr* 1E **19**
Cunning Park. *S Ayr* 4E **19**
Cunningsburgh. *Shet* 4C **100**
Cunnister. *Shet* 2H **101**
Cupar. *Fife* 2C **42**
Cupar Muir. *Fife* 2C **42**
Currie. *Edin* 3D **33**
Cuthill. *E Lot* 2F **33**
Cutts. *Shet* 3B **100**
Cuttyhill. *Abers* 4F **81**


## D


Dacre. *Cumb* 4D **9**
Dail. *Arg* 4B **46**
Dail Beag. *W Isl* 2D **96**
Dail bho Dheas. *W Isl* 1F **97**
Dailly. *S Ayr* 1D **11**
Dail Mor. *W Isl* 2D **96**
Dairsie. *Fife* 2D **43**
Dalabrog. *W Isl* 5G **93**
Dalavich. *Arg* 2A **38**
Dalbeattie. *Dum* 1D **7**
Dalblair. *E Ayr* 4B **20**
Dalchalm. *High* 3E **85**
Dalcharn. *High* 2B **88**
Dalchork. *High* 2A **84**
Dalchreichart. *High* 4F **65**
Dalchruin. *Per* 2C **40**
Dalcross. *High* 1E **67**
Dale. *Cumb* 3E **9**
Dalelia. *High* 1E **45**
Dale of Walls. *Shet* 1A **100**
Dalgarven. *N Ayr* 1D **19**
**Dalgety Bay**. *Fife* 1D **33**
Dalginross. *Per* 1C **40**
Dalguise. *Per* 3E **49**
Dalhalvaig. *High* 2D **89**
Dalintart. *Arg* 1F **37**
**Dalkeith**. *Midl* 3F **33**
Dallas. *Mor* 4C **78**
Dalleagles. *E Ayr* 4A **20**
Dall House. *Per* 2A **48**
Dalmally. *Arg* 1C **38**
Dalmarnock. *Glas* 3E **31**
Dalmellington. *E Ayr* 1F **11**
Dalmeny. *Edin* 2D **33**
Dalmigavie. *High* 4E **67**
Dalmilling. *S Ayr* 3E **19**
Dalmore. *High* 3D **77**
(nr. Alness)
Dalmore. *High* 3C **84**
(nr. Rogart)
Dalmuir. *W Dun* 2C **30**
Dalmunach. *Mor* 1D **69**
Dalnabreck. *High* 1E **45**
Dalnacardoch Lodge. *Per* 4E **57**
Dalnamein Lodge. *Per* 1C **48**
Dalnaspidal Lodge. *Per* 4D **57**
Dalnatrat. *High* 2A **46**
Dalnavie. *High* 2D **77**
Dalnawillan Lodge. *High* 3F **89**
Dalness. *High* 2C **46**
Dalnessie. *High* 2B **84**
Dalqueich. *Per* 3F **41**
Dalquhairn. *S Ayr* 2E **11**
Dalreavoch. *High* 3C **84**
Dalreoch. *Per* 2F **41**
Dalry. *Edin* 2E **33**
Dalry. *N Ayr* 1D **19**
Dalrymple. *E Ayr* 4E **19**
Dalserf. *S Lan* 4A **32**
Dalsmirren. *Arg* 4D **17**

| | | | |
|---|---|---|---|
| Dalston. *Cumb* | .2C 8 | Dron. *Per* | .2A 42 |
| Dalswinton. *Dum* | .3E 13 | Drongan. *E Ayr* | .4F 19 |
| Dalton. *Dum* | .4A 14 | Dronley. *Ang* | .4C 50 |
| Dalton. *S Lan* | .4E 31 | Druim. *High* | .4A 78 |
| Daltot. *Arg* | .1B 28 | Druimarbin. *High* | .4D 55 |
| Dalvey. *High* | .2C 68 | Druim Fhearna. *High* | .4F 63 |
| Dalwhinnie. *High* | .3D 57 | Druimindarroch. *High* | .3F 53 |
| Damhead. *Mor* | .4B 78 | Druim Saighdinis. *W Isl* | .1H 93 |
| Danderhall. *Midl* | .3F 33 | Drum. *Per* | .3F 41 |
| Danestone. *Aber* | .4E 71 | Drumbeg. *High* | .4C 86 |
| Dargill. *Per* | .2D 41 | Drumblade. *Abers* | .1A 70 |
| Darnford. *Abers* | .2C 60 | Drumbuie. *Dum* | .3A 12 |
| Darnick. *Bord* | .2E 23 | Drumbuie. *High* | .2A 64 |
| Darra. *Abers* | .1C 70 | Drumburgh. *Cumb* | .2B 8 |
| Dartfield. *Abers* | .4F 81 | Drumburn. *Dum* | .1E 7 |
| Darvel. *E Ayr* | .2A 20 | Drumchapel. *Glas* | .2D 31 |
| Dava. *Mor* | .2B 68 | Drumchardine. *High* | .1C 66 |
| Davidson's Mains. *Edin* | .2E 33 | Drumchork. *High* | .1B 74 |
| Davidston. *High* | .3E 77 | Drumclog. *S Lan* | .2B 20 |
| Davington. *Dum* | .1B 14 | Drumeldrie. *Fife* | .3D 43 |
| Daviot. *Abers* | .3C 70 | Drumfearn. *High* | .4F 63 |
| Daviot. *High* | .2E 67 | Drumgask. *High* | .2D 57 |
| Deadwater. *Nmbd* | .2F 15 | Drumgelloch. *N Lan* | .3F 31 |
| Dean. *Cumb* | .4F 7 | Drumguish. *High* | .2D 51 |
| Deanburnhaugh. *Bord* | .4C 22 | Drumin. *Mor* | .2C 68 |
| Deanich Lodge. *High* | .1A 76 | Drumindorsair. *High* | .1B 66 |
| Deans. *W Lot* | .3C 32 | Drumlamford House. *S Ayr* | .4D 11 |
| Deanscales. *Cumb* | .4F 7 | Drumlasie. *Abers* | .1B 60 |
| Deanston. *Stir* | .3C 40 | Drumlemble. *Arg* | .4D 17 |
| Dearham. *Cumb* | .4F 7 | Drumlithie. *Abers* | .3C 60 |
| Dechmont. *W Lot* | .2C 32 | Drummoddie. *Dum* | .3E 5 |
| Deebank. *Abers* | .2B 60 | Drummore. *Dum* | .3D 77 |
| Deerhill. *Mor* | .4F 79 | Drummuir. *Mor* | .1E 69 |
| Deerness. *Orkn* | .2D 98 | Drumnadrochit. *High* | .2C 66 |
| Delfour. *High* | .1F 57 | Drumrunie. *High* | .3C 82 |
| Delliefure. *High* | .2B 68 | Drumry. *W Dun* | .2D 31 |
| Delny. *High* | .2E 77 | Drums. *Abers* | .3E 71 |
| Den, The. *N Ayr* | .4B 30 | Drumsleet. *Dum* | .4E 13 |
| Denbeath. *Fife* | .4C 42 | Drumsmittal. *High* | .1D 67 |
| Denhead. *Abers* | .2E 71 | Drums of Park. *Abers* | .4A 80 |
| (nr. Ellon) | | Drumsturdy. *Ang* | .4D 51 |
| Denhead. *Abers* | .4E 81 | Drumuie. *High* | .1D 63 |
| (nr. Strichen) | | Drumuillie. *High* | .3A 68 |
| Denhead. *Fife* | .2D 43 | Drumvaich. *Stir* | .3B 40 |
| Denholm. *Bord* | .4E 23 | Drumwhindle. *Abers* | .2E 71 |
| Denny. *Falk* | .1A 32 | Drunkendub. *Ang* | .3F 51 |
| Dennyloanhead. *Falk* | .1A 32 | Dry Harbour. *High* | .4E 63 |
| Den of Lindores. *Fife* | .2B 42 | Dryburgh. *Bord* | .2E 23 |
| Denside. *Abers* | .2D 61 | Drymen. *Stir* | .1C 30 |
| Denwick. *Nmbd* | .4F 25 | Drymuir. *Abers* | .1E 71 |
| Derculich. *Per* | .2D 49 | Drynie Park. *High* | .4C 76 |
| Derryguaig. *Arg* | .4B 44 | Drynoch. *High* | .3C 80 |
| Dervaig. *Arg* | .2B 44 | Dubford. *Abers* | .3C 80 |
| Detchant. *Nmbd* | .2D 25 | Dubton. *Abers* | .4B 80 |
| Deuchar. *Ang* | .1D 51 | Dubton. *Ang* | .2E 51 |
| Devonside. *Clac* | .4E 41 | Duchally. *High* | .2F 83 |
| Dewartown. *Midl* | .3F 33 | Duddingston. *Edin* | .2E 33 |
| Digg. *High* | .3D 73 | Duddo. *Nmbd* | .1C 24 |
| Dillarburn. *S Lan* | .1D 21 | Dufftown. *Mor* | .1E 69 |
| Dingleton. *Bord* | .2E 23 | Duffus. *Mor* | .2D 79 |
| Dingwall. *High* | .4C 76 | Dufton. *Cumb* | .4F 9 |
| Dinnet. *Abers* | .2F 59 | Duirinish. *High* | .2A 64 |
| Dippen. *Arg* | .2E 17 | Duisdalemore. *High* | .4F 63 |
| Dippin. *N Ayr* | .3B 18 | Duisdeil Mòr. *High* | .4F 63 |
| Dipple. *S Ayr* | .1D 11 | Duisky. *High* | .4D 55 |
| Dirleton. *E Lot* | .1B 34 | Dull. *Per* | .3D 49 |
| Dishes. *Orkn* | .5H 99 | Dullatur. *N Lan* | .2F 31 |
| Distington. *Cumb* | .4F 7 | Dulnain Bridge. *High* | .3A 68 |
| Divach. *High* | .3B 66 | Dumfin. *Arg* | .1C 30 |
| Dixonfield. *High* | .1A 90 | Dumbarton. *W Dun* | .2C 30 |
| Dochgarroch. *High* | .1D 67 | Dumfries. *Dum* | .103 (4E 13) |
| Doddington. *Nmbd* | .2C 24 | Dumgoyne. *Stir* | .1D 31 |
| Doll. *High* | .3D 85 | Dun. *Ang* | .1F 51 |
| Dollar. *Clac* | .4E 41 | Dunagoil. *Arg* | .4E 29 |
| Dolphinton. *S Lan* | .1A 22 | Dunalastair. *Per* | .2C 48 |
| Doonfoot. *S Ayr* | .4E 19 | Dunan. *High* | .3E 63 |
| Doonholm. *S Ayr* | .4E 19 | Dunbar. *E Lot* | .2C 34 |
| Dorback Lodge. *High* | .4B 68 | Dunbeath. *High* | .4A 90 |
| Dores. *High* | .2C 66 | Dunbeg. *Arg* | .4F 45 |
| Dornie. *High* | .3B 64 | Dunblane. *Stir* | .3C 40 |
| Dornoch. *High* | .1E 77 | Dunbog. *Fife* | .2B 42 |
| Dornock. *Dum* | .1B 8 | Duncanston. *Abers* | .3A 70 |
| Dorrery. *High* | .2F 89 | Duncanston. *High* | .4C 76 |
| Dougarie. *N Ayr* | .2F 17 | Dun Charlabhaigh. *W Isl* | .2C 96 |
| Douglas. *S Lan* | .2D 21 | Duncow. *Dum* | .3E 13 |
| Douglastown. *Ang* | .3D 51 | Duncrievie. *Per* | .3A 42 |
| Douglas Water. *S Lan* | .2D 21 | Dundee. *D'dee* | .103 (4D 51) |
| Dounby. *Orkn* | .1A 98 | Dundee Airport. *D'dee* | .1C 42 |
| Doune. *High* | .4F 67 | Dundonald. *S Ayr* | .2E 19 |
| (nr. Kingussie) | | Dundonnell. *High* | .1D 75 |
| Doune. *High* | .3F 83 | Dundraw. *Cumb* | .3B 8 |
| (nr. Lairg) | | Dundreggan. *High* | .4A 66 |
| Doune. *Stir* | .3C 40 | Dundrennan. *Dum* | .3C 6 |
| Dounie. *High* | .4A 84 | Dunecht. *Abers* | .1C 60 |
| (nr. Bonar Bridge) | | Dunfermline. *Fife* | .103 (1C 32) |
| Dounie. *High* | .1D 77 | Dunino. *Fife* | .2E 43 |
| (nr. Tain) | | Dunipace. *Falk* | .1A 32 |
| Dounreay. *High* | .1E 89 | Dunira. *Per* | .1C 40 |
| Doura. *N Ayr* | .1E 19 | Dunkeld. *Per* | .3F 49 |
| Dovenby. *Cumb* | .4F 7 | Dunlappie. *Ang* | .1E 51 |
| Dowally. *Per* | .3F 49 | Dunlichity Lodge. *High* | .2D 67 |
| Downfield. *D'dee* | .4C 50 | Dunlop. *E Ayr* | .1F 19 |
| Downham. *Nmbd* | .2B 24 | Dunmaglass Lodge. *High* | .3C 66 |
| Downies. *Abers* | .2E 61 | Dunmore. *Arg* | .3B 28 |
| Doxford. *Nmbd* | .3E 25 | Dunmore. *Falk* | .1A 32 |
| Draffan. *S Lan* | .1C 20 | | |
| Drakemyre. *N Ayr* | .4A 30 | | |
| Dreghorn. *N Ayr* | .2E 19 | | |
| Drem. *E Lot* | .2B 34 | | |
| Dreumasdal. *W Isl* | .4G 93 | | |
| Drimnin. *High* | .2C 44 | | |
| Drinisiadar. *W Isl* | .3F 95 | | |
| Droman. *High* | .2C 86 | | |

| | | | |
|---|---|---|---|
| Dunmore. *High* | .1C 66 | East Rhidorroch Lodge. | |
| Dunnet. *High* | .5A 98 | High | .4D 83 |
| Dunnichen. *Ang* | .3E 51 | Eastriggs. *Dum* | .1B 8 |
| Dunning. *Per* | .2F 41 | East Saltoun. *E Lot* | .3A 34 |
| **Dunoon.** *Arg* | .2F 29 | Eastshore. *Shet* | .5B 100 |
| Dunphail. *Mor* | .1B 68 | East Wemyss. *Fife* | .4C 42 |
| Dunragit. *Dum* | .2C 4 | East Whitburn. *W Lot* | .3B 32 |
| Dunrostan. *Arg* | .1B 28 | Eastwick. *Shet* | .4F 101 |
| Duns. *Bord* | .4D 35 | Ecclefechan. *Dum* | .4A 14 |
| Dunscore. *Dum* | .3D 13 | Eccles. *Bord* | .1A 24 |
| Dunshalt. *Fife* | .2B 42 | Ecclesmachan. *W Lot* | .2C 32 |
| Dunshillock. *Abers* | .1E 71 | Echt. *Abers* | .1C 60 |
| Dunstan. *Nmbd* | .4F 25 | Eckford. *Bord* | .3A 24 |
| Dunsyre. *S Lan* | .1F 21 | Eday Airport. *Orkn* | .4G 99 |
| Duntocher. *W Dun* | .2C 30 | Edderside. *Cumb* | .3A 8 |
| Duntulm. *High* | .1D 62 | Edderton. *High* | .1E 77 |
| Dunure. *S Ayr* | .4D 19 | Eddleston. *Bord* | .1B 22 |
| Dunvegan. *High* | .1B 62 | Eddlewood. *S Lan* | .4F 31 |
| Durdar. *Cumb* | .2D 9 | Edendonich. *High* | .1C 38 |
| Durisdeer. *Dum* | .1D 13 | Edenhall. *Cumb* | .4E 9 |
| Durisdeermill. *Dum* | .1D 13 | Edentaggart. *Arg* | .4E 39 |
| Durnamuck. *High* | .4B 82 | Edgehead. *Midl* | .3F 33 |
| Durness. *High* | .1F 87 | Edinbane. *High* | .4C 72 |
| Durno. *Abers* | .3C 70 | **Edinburgh.** *Edin* | .104 (2E 33) |
| Duror. *High* | .2A 46 | Edinburgh Airport. | |
| Durran. *Arg* | .3A 38 | Edin | .2D 33 |
| Durran. *High* | .1A 90 | Edingham. *Nmbd* | .4E 25 |
| Dury. *Shet* | .1C 100 | Edmonstone. *Orkn* | .5G 99 |
| Duthil. *High* | .3A 68 | Ednam. *Bord* | .2A 24 |
| Dyce. *Aber* | .4D 71 | Edrom. *Bord* | .4E 35 |
| Dyke. *Mor* | .4A 78 | Edzell. *Ang* | .1F 51 |
| Dykehead. *Ang* | .1C 50 | Effirth. *Shet* | .1B 100 |
| Dykehead. *N Lan* | .3A 32 | Efstigarth. *Shet* | .2G 101 |
| Dykehead. *Stir* | .4A 40 | Eglingham. *Nmbd* | .4E 25 |
| Dykend. *Ang* | .2B 50 | Eight Mile Burn. *Midl* | .4D 33 |
| Dykesfield. *Cumb* | .2C 8 | Eignaig. *High* | .3E 45 |
| Dysart. *Fife* | .4C 42 | Eilanreach. *High* | .4B 64 |

Longpark—Newbie


Longpark. *Cumb* 1D **9**
Longridge. *W Lot* 3B **32**
Longriggend. *N Lan* 2A **32**
Longside. *Abers* 1F **71**
Longtown. *Cumb* 1C **8**
Longyester. *E Lot* 3B **34**
Lonmore. *High* 1B **62**
Lorbottle. *Nmbd* 4D **25**
Losgaintir. *W Isl* 3E **95**
Lossiemouth. *Mor* 3D **79**
Lossit. *Arg* 4B **26**
Lothbeg. *High* 2E **85**
Lothianbridge. *Midl* 3F **33**
Lothianburn. *Midl* 3E **33**
Lothmore. *High* 2E **85**
Low Ardwell. *Dum* 3B **4**
Low Ballochdowan. *S Ayr* 4B **10**
Low Braithwaite. *Cumb* 3D **9**
Low Coylton. *S Ayr* 4F **19**
Low Crosby. *Cumb* 2D **9**
Lower Arboll. *High* 1F **77**
Lower Auchenreath. *Mor* 3E **79**
Lower Badcall. *High* 3C **86**
Lower Breakish. *High* 3F **63**
Lower Diabaig. *High* 3A **74**
Lower Dounreay. *High* 1E **89**
Lower Gledfield. *High* 4A **84**
Lower Killeyan. *Arg* 1A **16**
Lower Largo. *Fife* 3D **43**
Lower Lenie. *High* 3C **66**
Lower Milovaig. *High* 4A **72**
Lower Oakfield. *Fife* 4A **42**
Lower Ollach. *High* 2E **63**
Lower Pitkerrie. *High* 2F **77**
Lowertown. *Orkn* 3C **98**
Low Hesket. *Cumb* 3D **9**
Lowick. *Nmbd* 2D **25**
Low Lorton. *Cumb* 4A **8**
Low Newton-by-the-Sea. *Nmbd* 3F **25**
Lownie Moor. *Ang* 3D **51**
Lowood. *Bord* 2E **23**
Low Row. *Cumb* 1E **9** (nr. Brampton)
Low Row. *Cumb* 3A **8** (nr. Wigton)
Low Torry. *Fife* 1C **32**
Low Valleyfield. *Fife* 1B **32**
Low Whinnow. *Cumb* 2C **8**
Lubcroy. *High* 3E **83**
Lubinvullin. *High* 1A **88**
Lucker. *Nmbd* 2E **25**
Lucklawhill. *Fife* 1D **43**
Ludag. *W Isl* 1C **92**
Lugar. *E Ayr* 3A **20**
Luggate Burn. *E Lot* 2C **34**
Luggiebank. *N Lan* 2F **31**
Lugton. *E Ayr* 4C **30**
Luib. *High* 3E **63**
Luib. *Stir* 1F **39**
Lumphanan. *Abers* 1A **60**
Lumphinnans. *Fife* 4A **42**
Lumsdaine. *Bord* 3E **35**
Lumsden. *Abers* 3F **69**
Lunan. *Ang* 2F **51**
Lunanhead. *Ang* 2D **51**
Luncarty. *Per* 1F **41**
Lundie. *Ang* 4B **50**
Lundin Links. *Fife* 3D **43**
Lunna. *Shet* 5G **101**
Lunning. *Shet* 5H **101**
Luss. *Arg* 4E **39**
Lussagiven. *Arg* 1A **28**
Lusta. *High* 4B **72**
Luthermuir. *Abers* 1F **51**
Luthrie. *Fife* 2C **42**
Lybster. *High* 4B **90**
Lyham. *Nmbd* 2D **25**
Lylestone. *N Ayr* 1E **19**
Lynaberack Lodge. *High* 2E **57**
Lynchat. *High* 1E **57**
Lyne. *Bord* 1B **22**
Lyneholmeford. *Cumb* 4E **15**
Lyne of Gorthleck. *High* 3C **66**
Lyne of Skene. *Abers* 4C **70**
Lyness. *Orkn* 3B **98**
Lynwilg. *High* 4F **67**
Lyth. *High* 1B **90**
Lythes. *Orkn* 4C **98**
Lythmore. *High* 1F **89**

## M

Mabie. *Dum* 4E **13**
Macbiehill. *Bord* 4D **33**
Macduff. *Abers* 3C **80**
Machan. *S Lan* 4F **31**
Macharioch. *Arg* 4E **17**
Machrie. *N Ayr* 2F **17**
Machrihanish. *Arg* 3D **17**
Macmerry. *E Lot* 2A **34**
Madderty. *Per* 1E **41**
Maddiston. *Falk* 2B **32**
Maggieknockater. *Mor* 1E **69**
Maidens. *S Ayr* 1D **11**
Mail. *Shet* 4C **100**
Mains of Auchindachy. *Mor* 1F **69**
Mains of Auchnagatt. *Abers* 1E **71**
Mains of Drum. *Abers* 2D **61**
Mains of Edingight. *Mor* 4A **80**
Mainsriddle. *Dum* 2E **7**
Makerstoun. *Bord* 2F **23**
Malacleit. *W Isl* 5B **94**
Malaig. *High* 2F **53**
Malaig Bheag. *High* 2F **53**
Malcolmburn. *Mor* 4E **79**
Maligar. *High* 3D **73**
**Mallaig**. *High* 2F **53**
Malleny Mills. *Edin* 3D **33**
Malt Lane. *Arg* 3B **38**
Manais. *W Isl* 4F **95**
Mangurstadh. *W Isl* 3B **96**
Mannal. *Arg* 3E **91**
Mannerston. *Falk* 2C **32**
Mannofield. *Aber* 1E **61**
Mansewood. *Glas* 3D **31**
Mansfield. *E Ayr* 4B **20**
Maraig. *W Isl* 2G **95**
Marbhig. *W Isl* 5F **97**
Margnaheglish. *N Ayr* 2B **18**
Marishader. *High* 3D **73**
Marjoriebanks. *Dum* 3F **13**
Mark. *Dum* 2C **4**
Markethill. *Per* 4B **50**
Markinch. *Fife* 3B **42**
Mar Lodge. *Abers* 3B **58**
Marnoch. *Abers* 4A **80**
Marnock. *N Lan* 3F **31**
Marrel. *High* 2F **85**
Marrister. *Shet* 5H **101**
Marshall Meadows. *Nmbd* 4F **35**
Marwick. *Orkn* 1A **98**
Marybank. *High* 4B **76** (nr. Dingwall)
Marybank. *High* 2E **77** (nr. Invergordon)
Maryburgh. *High* 4C **76**
Maryhill. *Glas* 3D **31**
Marykirk. *Abers* 1F **51**
Marypark. *Mor* 2C **68**
**Maryport**. *Cumb* 4F **7**
Maryport. *Dum* 4C **4**
Maryton. *Ang* 2C **50** (nr. Kirriemuir)
Maryton. *Ang* 2F **51** (nr. Montrose)
Marywell. *Abers* 2A **60**
Marywell. *Ang* 3F **51**
Masons Lodge. *Abers* 1D **61**
Mastrick. *Aber* 1E **61**
Matterdale End. *Cumb* 4C **8**
Mauchline. *E Ayr* 3F **19**
Maud. *Abers* 1E **71**
Mawbray. *Cumb* 3F **7**
Maxton. *Bord* 2F **23**
Maxwellheugh. *Bord* 2A **24**
Maxwelltown. *Dum* 4E **13**
Maybole. *S Ayr* 1E **11**
**Mayfield**. *Midl* 3F **33**
Mayfield. *Per* 1F **41**
Maywick. *Shet* 4B **100**
Meadowmill. *E Lot* 2A **34**
Mealabost. *W Isl* 1F **97** (nr. Borgh)
Mealabost. *W Isl* 3F **97** (nr. Stornoway)
Mealasta. *W Isl* 4A **96**
Mealrigg. *Cumb* 3A **8**
Mealsgate. *Cumb* 3B **8**
Meigle. *Per* 3B **50**
Meikle Earnock. *S Lan* 4F **31**
Meikle Kilchattan Butts. *Arg* 4E **29**
Meikleour. *Per* 4A **50**
Meikle Tarty. *Abers* 3E **71**
Meikle Wartle. *Abers* 2C **70**
Melby. *Shet* 1A **100**
Melfort. *Arg* 2F **37**
Melgarve. *High* 2B **56**
Melkington. *Nmbd* 1B **24**
Melkinthorpe. *Cumb* 4E **9**
Melkridge. *Nmbd* 1F **9**
Mellangaun. *High* 1B **74**
Melldalloch. *Arg* 2D **29**
Mellguards. *Cumb* 3D **9**
Mellon Charles. *High* 1B **74**
Mellon Udrigle. *High* 1B **74**
Melmerby. *Cumb* 4F **9**
Melrose. *Bord* 2E **23**
Melsetter. *Orkn* 4A **98**
Melvaig. *High* 1A **74**
Melvich. *High* 1D **89**
Memsie. *Abers* 3E **81**
Memus. *Ang* 2D **51**
Mennock. *Dum* 1D **13**
Menstrie. *Clac* 4D **41**
Merchiston. *Edin* 2E **33**
Merkadale. *High* 2C **62**
Merkland. *S Ayr* 2D **11**
Merkland Lodge. *High* 1E **83**
Methil. *Fife* 4C **42**
Methilhill. *Fife* 4C **42**
Methlick. *Abers* 2D **71**
Methven. *Per* 1F **41**
Mey. *High* 5A **98**
Miabhag. *W Isl* 3F **95**
Miabhaig. *W Isl* 2E **95** (nr. Cliasmol)
Miabhaig. *W Isl* 3B **96** (nr. Timsgearraidh)
Mial. *High* 2A **74**
Micklethwaite. *Cumb* 2B **8**
Mid Ardlaw. *Abers* 3E **81**
Midbea. *Orkn* 3F **99**
Mid Beltie. *Abers* 1B **60**
Mid Calder. *W Lot* 3C **32**
Mid Clyth. *High* 4B **90**
Middlebie. *Dum* 4B **14**
Middle Drums. *Ang* 2E **51**
Middle Essie. *Abers* 4F **81**
Middlemuir. *Abers* 1D **71** (nr. New Deer)
Middlemuir. *Abers* 4E **81** (nr. Strichen)
Middlesceugh. *Cumb* 3C **8**
Middleton. *Ang* 3E **51**
Middleton. *Arg* 3E **91**
Middleton. *Midl* 4F **33**
Middleton. *Nmbd* 2E **25**
Middleton. *Per* 3A **42**
Midfield. *High* 1A **88**
Mid Garrary. *Dum* 4A **12**
Midgeholme. *Cumb* 2F **9**
Mid Ho. *Shet* 2H **101**
Mid Kirkton. *N Ayr* 4F **29**
Midland. *Orkn* 2B **98**
Midlem. *Bord* 3E **23**
Midton. *Inv* 2A **30**
Midtown. *High* 1B **74** (nr. Poolewe)
Midtown. *High* 1A **88** (nr. Tongue)
Mid Walls. *Shet* 2A **100**
Mid Yell. *Shet* 2H **101**
Migdale. *High* 4B **84**
Migvie. *Abers* 1F **59**
Milburn. *Cumb* 4F **9**
Milesmark. *Fife* 1C **32**
Milfield. *Nmbd* 2C **24**
Millbank. *High* 1A **90**
Millbeck. *Cumb* 4B **8**
Millbounds. *Orkn* 4G **99**
Millbreck. *Abers* 1F **71**
Millden Lodge. *Ang* 4A **60**
Milldens. *Ang* 2E **51**
Millearn. *Per* 2E **41**
Millerhill. *Midl* 3F **33**
Millerston. *Glas* 3E **31**
Millfield. *Abers* 2F **59**
Millhall. *E Ren* 4D **31**
Millheugh. *S Lan* 4F **31**
Millhouse. *Arg* 2D **29**
Millhouse. *Cumb* 4C **8**
Millhousebridge. *Dum* 3A **14**
Millikenpark. *Ren* 3C **30**
Mill Knowe. *Arg* 3E **17**
Mill of Craigievar. *Abers* 4A **70**
Mill of Fintray. *Abers* 4D **71**
Mill of Haldane. *W Dun* 1C **30**
Millport. *N Ayr* 4F **29**
Milltimber. *Aber* 1D **61**
Milltown. *Abers* 1D **59** (nr. Corgarff)
Milltown. *Abers* 4F **69** (nr. Lumsden)
Milltown. *Dum* 4C **14**
Milltown of Aberdalgie. *Per* 1F **41**
Milltown of Auchindoun. *Mor* 1E **69**
Milltown of Campfield. *Abers* 1B **60**
Milltown of Edinvillie. *Mor* 1D **69**
Milltown of Rothiemay. *Mor* 1A **70**
Milltown of Towie. *Abers* 4F **69**
Milnacraig. *Ang* 2B **50**
Milnathort. *Per* 3A **42**
**Milngavie**. *E Dun* 2D **31**
Milnholm. *Stir* 1F **31**
Milton. *Ang* 3C **50**
Milton. *Cumb* 1E **9**
Milton. *Dum* 4D **13** (nr. Crocketford)
Milton. *Dum* 2D **5** (nr. Glenluce)
Milton. *Glas* 3D **31**
Milton. *High* 4A **76** (nr. Achnasheen)
Milton. *High* 1A **64** (nr. Applecross)
Milton. *High* 2B **66** (nr. Drumnadrochit)
Milton. *High* 2E **77** (nr. Invergordon)
Milton. *High* 1C **66** (nr. Inverness)
Milton. *High* 2C **90** (nr. Wick)
Milton. *Mor* 3A **80** (nr. Cullen)
Milton. *Mor* 4C **68** (nr. Tomintoul)
Milton. *S Ayr* 3F **19**
Milton. *Stir* 3A **40** (nr. Aberfoyle)
Milton. *Stir* 4F **39** (nr. Drymen)
Milton. *W Dun* 2C **30**
Milton Auchlossan. *Abers* 1A **60**
Milton Bridge. *Midl* 3E **33**
Milton Coldwells. *Abers* 2E **71**
Miltonduff. *Mor* 3C **78**
Milton Morenish. *Per* 4B **48**
Milton of Auchinhove. *Abers* 1A **60**
Milton of Balgonie. *Fife* 3C **42**
Milton of Barras. *Abers* 4D **61**
Milton of Campsie. *E Dun* 2E **31**
Milton of Cultoquhey. *Per* 1D **41**
Milton of Cushnie. *Abers* 4A **70**
Milton of Finavon. *Ang* 2D **51**
Milton of Gollanfield. *High* 4E **77**
Milton of Lesmore. *Abers* 3F **69**
Milton of Leys. *High* 1D **67**
Milton of Tullich. *Abers* 2E **59**
Minard. *Arg* 4A **38**
Mindrum. *Nmbd* 2B **24**
Mingarrypark. *High* 1D **45**
Mingary. *High* 1C **44**
Mingearraidh. *W Isl* 5G **93**
Minishant. *S Ayr* 4E **19**
Minnigaff. *Dum* 1F **5**
Mintlaw. *Abers* 1F **71**
Minto. *Bord* 3E **23**
Miodar. *Arg* 3F **91**
Mirbister. *Orkn* 5E **99**
Mireland. *High* 1C **90**
Moaness. *Orkn* 2A **98**
Moarfield. *Shet* 1H **101**
Moat. *Cumb* 4D **15**
Mochrum. *Dum* 3E **5**
Modsarie. *High* 1B **88**
Moffat. *Dum* 1F **13**
Mol-chlach. *High* 4D **63**
Moll. *High* 3E **63**
Mollinsburn. *N Lan* 2F **31**
Monachyle. *Stir* 2F **39**
Monar Lodge. *High* 1F **65**
Moneydie. *Per* 1F **41**
Moniaive. *Dum* 2C **12**
Monifieth. *Ang* 4E **51**
Monikie. *Ang* 4E **51**
Monimail. *Fife* 2B **42**
Monkhill. *Cumb* 2C **8**
Monkshill. *Abers* 1C **70**
Monkton. *S Ayr* 3E **19**
Monktonhill. *S Ayr* 3E **19**
Monreith. *Dum* 3E **5**
Montford. *Arg* 3F **29**
Montgarrie. *Abers* 4A **70**
Montgarswood. *E Ayr* 3A **20**
Montgreenan. *N Ayr* 1E **19**
Montrave. *Fife* 3C **42**
**Montrose**. *Ang* 2F **51**
Monymusk. *Abers* 4B **70**
Monzie. *Per* 1D **41**
Moodiesburn. *N Lan* 2E **31**
Moonzie. *Fife* 2C **42**
Moorbrae. *Shet* 3G **101**
Moorend. *Dum* 4B **14**
Moorhouse. *Cumb* 2C **8** (nr. Carlisle)
Moorhouse. *Cumb* 2B **8** (nr. Wigton)
Moor of Granary. *Mor* 4B **78**
Moor Row. *Cumb* 3B **8**
Morangie. *High* 1E **77**
Morar. *High* 2F **53**
Morebattle. *Bord* 3A **24**
Morefield. *High* 4C **82**
Morenish. *Per* 4A **48**
Morham. *E Lot* 2B **34**
Morningside. *Edin* 2E **33**
Morningside. *N Lan* 4A **32**
Morrington. *Dum* 3D **13**
Morton. *Cumb* 4D **9** (nr. Calthwaite)
Morton. *Cumb* 2C **8** (nr. Carlisle)
Morvich. *High* 3C **84** (nr. Golspie)
Morvich. *High* 3C **64** (nr. Shiel Bridge)
Morwick. *Nmbd* 4F **25**
Moscow. *E Ayr* 1F **19**
Mosedale. *Cumb* 4C **8**
Moss. *Arg* 3E **91**
Moss. *High* 1D **45**
Mossatt. *Abers* 4F **69**
Mossbank. *Shet* 4G **101**
Mossblown. *S Ayr* 3F **19**
Mossburnford. *Bord* 4F **23**
Mossdale. *Dum* 4B **12**
Mossedge. *Cumb* 1D **9**
Mossend. *N Lan* 3F **31**
Moss of Barmuckity. *Mor* 3D **79**
Mosspark. *Glas* 3D **31**
Mosspaul. *Bord* 2D **15**
Moss Side. *Cumb* 2A **8**
Moss-side. *High* 4F **77**
Moss-side of Cairness. *Abers* 3F **81**
Mosstodloch. *Mor* 3E **79**
Motherby. *Cumb* 4D **9**
**Motherwell**. *N Lan* **106 (4F 31)**
Moulin. *Per* 2E **49**
Mountain Cross. *Bord* 1A **22**
Mountbenger. *Bord* 3C **22**
Mountblow. *W Dun* 2C **30**
Mountgerald. *High* 3C **76**
Mount High. *High* 3D **77**
Mount Lothian. *Midl* 4E **33**
Mount Stuart. *Arg* 4F **29**
Mouswald. *Dum* 4F **13**
Mowhaugh. *Bord* 3B **24**
Moy. *High* 2E **67**
Moy Lodge. *High* 3B **56**
Muasdale. *Arg* 1D **17**
Muchalls. *Abers* 2E **61**
Muchrachd. *High* 2F **65**
Muckle Breck. *Shet* 5H **101**
Mudale. *High* 4A **88**
Mugdock. *Stir* 2D **31**
Mugeary. *High* 2D **63**
Muie. *High* 3B **84**
Muirden. *Abers* 4C **80**
Muirdrum. *Ang* 4E **51**
Muiredge. *Per* 1B **42**
Muirend. *Glas* 3D **31**
Muirhead. *Ang* 4C **50**
Muirhead. *Fife* 3B **42**
Muirhead. *N Lan* 3E **31**
Muirhouses. *Falk* 1C **32**
Muirkirk. *E Ayr* 3B **20**
Muir of Alford. *Abers* 4A **70**
Muir of Fairburn. *High* 4B **76**
Muir of Fowlis. *Abers* 4A **70**
Muir of Miltonduff. *Mor* 4C **78**
Muir of Ord. *High* 4C **76**
Muir of Tarradale. *High* 4C **76**
Muirshearlich. *High* 3E **55**
Muirtack. *Abers* 2E **71**
Muirton. *High* 3E **77**
Muirton. *Per* 1A **42**
Muirton of Ardblair. *Per* 3A **50**
Muirtown. *Per* 2E **41**
Muiryfold. *Abers* 4C **80**
Mulben. *Mor* 4E **79**
Mulindry. *Arg* 4D **27**
Mulla. *Shet* 5G **101**
Mullach Charlabhaigh. *W Isl* 2D **96**
Munerigie. *High* 1F **55**
Muness. *Shet* 1H **101**
Mungasdale. *High* 4A **82**
Mungrisdale. *Cumb* 4C **8**
Munlochy. *High* 4D **77**
Murieston. *W Lot* 3C **32**
Murkle. *High* 1A **90**
Murlaggan. *High* 2D **55**
Murra. *Orkn* 2A **98**
Murray, The. *S Lan* 4E **31**
Murrayfield. *Edin* 2E **33**
Murroes. *Ang* 4D **51**
Murthly. *Per* 4F **49**
Murton. *Nmbd* 1C **24**
**Musselburgh**. *E Lot* 2F **33**
Mutehill. *Dum* 3B **6**
Muthill. *Per* 2D **41**
Mybster. *High* 2A **90**
Myrebird. *Abers* 2C **60**
Myrelandhorn. *High* 2B **90**

## N

Naast. *High* 1B **74**
Na Buirgh. *W Isl* 3E **95**
Na Gearrannan. *W Isl* 2C **96**
Nairn. *High* 4F **77**
Navidale. *High* 2F **85**
Nealhouse. *Cumb* 2C **8**
Nedd. *High* 4C **86**
Neilston. *E Ren* 4C **30**
Nemphlar. *S Lan* 1D **21**
Nenthall. *Cumb* 3F **9**
Nenthorn. *Bord* 2F **23**
Neribus. *Arg* 4C **26**
Nerston. *S Lan* 4E **31**
Nesbit. *Nmbd* 2C **24**
Ness of Tenston. *Orkn* 1A **98**
Nethanfoot. *S Lan* 1D **21**
Nether Blainslie. *Bord* 1E **23**
Netherbrae. *Abers* 4C **80**
Netherbrough. *Orkn* 1B **98**
Netherburn. *S Lan* 1D **21**
Netherby. *Cumb* 4C **14**
Nether Careston. *Ang* 2E **51**
Nether Dallachy. *Mor* 3E **79**
Nether Durdie. *Per* 1B **42**
Nether Howcleugh. *S Lan* 4F **21**
Nether Kinmundy. *Abers* 1F **71**
Netherlaw. *Dum* 3C **6**
Netherley. *Abers* 2D **61**
Nethermill. *Dum* 3F **13**
Nethermills. *Mor* 4A **80**
Netherplace. *E Ren* 4D **31**
Netherthird. *E Ayr* 4A **20**
Netherton. *Ang* 2E **51**
Netherton. *Cumb* 4F **7**
Netherton. *N Lan* 4F **31**
Netherton. *Nmbd* 4C **24**
Netherton. *Per* 2A **50**
Netherton. *Stir* 2D **31**
Nethertown. *High* 5B **98**
Nether Urquhart. *Fife* 3A **42**
Nether Welton. *Cumb* 3C **8**
Nethy Bridge. *High* 3B **68**
Neuk, The. *Abers* 2C **60**
New Abbey. *Dum* 1E **7**
New Aberdour. *Abers* 3D **81**
New Alyth. *Per* 3B **50**
Newark. *Orkn* 3H **99**
Newarthill. *N Lan* 4F **31**
Newbattle. *Midl* 3F **33**
New Bewick. *Nmbd* 3D **25**
Newbie. *Dum* 1A **8**

Newbiggin—Ramstone


…4F **9**
(…pleby)
…3E **9**
(…Cumrew)
…4D **9**
(…nr. Penrith)
…4D **51**
(nr. Monikie)
…3B **50**
(nr. Newtyle)
…ng. *Ang* 4D **51**
(nr. Tealing)
…bigging. *Edin* 2D **33**
…bigging. *S Lan* 1F **21**
…ew Bridge. *Dum* 4E **13**
…ewbridge. *Edin* 2D **33**
…ewburgh. *Abers* 3E **71**
Newburgh. *Fife* 2B **42**
Newby East. *Cumb* 2D **9**
New Byth. *Abers* 4D **81**
Newby West. *Cumb* 2C **8**
Newcastleton. *Bord* 3D **15**
New Cowper. *Cumb* 3A **8**
Newcraighall. *Edin* 2F **33**
New Cumnock. *E Ayr* 4B **20**
New Deer. *Abers* 1D **71**
New Elgin. *Mor* 3D **79**
New Galloway. *Dum* 4B **12**
Newham. *Nmbd* 3E **25**
Newhaven. *Edin* 2E **33**
Newhouse. *N Lan* 3F **31**
Newington. *Edin* 2E **33**
New Kelso. *High* 1C **64**
New Lanark. *S Lan* 1D **21**
Newlandrig. *Midl* 3F **33**
Newlands. *Cumb* 4C **8**
Newlands. *High* 1E **67**
Newlands of Geise. *High* 1F **89**
Newlands of Tynet. *Mor* 3E **79**
New Langholm. *Dum* 3C **14**
New Leeds. *Abers* 4E **81**
Newlot. *Orkn* 1D **98**
New Luce. *Dum* 1C **4**
Newmachar. *Abers* 4D **71**
Newmains. *N Lan* 4A **32**
New Mains of Ury. *Abers* 3D **61**
Newmarket. *W Isl* 3F **97**
New Mill. *Abers* 1C **70**
Newmill. *Mor* 4F **79**
Newmill. *Bord* 4D **23**
Newmills. *Fife* 1C **32**
Newmills. *High* 3D **77**
Newmiln. *Per* 4A **50**
Newmilns. *E Ayr* 2A **20**
Newmore. *High* 4C **76**
(nr. Dingwall)
Newmore. *High* 2D **77**
(nr. Invergordon)
Newpark. *Fife* 2D **43**
New Pitsligo. *Abers* 4D **81**
Newport. *High* 1F **85**
Newport-on-Tay. *Fife* 1D **43**
New Prestwick. *S Ayr* 3E **19**
New Rent. *Cumb* 4D **9**
New Sauchie. *Clac* 4D **41**
Newseat. *Abers* 2C **70**
New Shoreston. *Nmbd* 2E **25**
Newstead. *Bord* 2E **23**
New Stevenston. *N Lan* 4F **31**
Newton. *Arg* 4B **38**
Newton. *Dum* 4B **14**
(nr. Annan)
Newton. *Dum* 2A **14**
(nr. Moffat)
Newton. *High* 3E **77**
(nr. Cromarty)
Newton. *High* 1E **67**
(nr. Inverness)
Newton. *High* 4D **87**
(nr. Kylestrome)
Newton. *High* 3C **90**
(nr. Wick)
Newton. *Mor* 3C **78**
Newton. *Bord* 3F **23**
Newton. *Shet* 3B **100**
Newton. *S Lan* 3E **31**
(nr. Glasgow)
Newton. *S Lan* 2E **21**
(nr. Lanark)
Newton. *W Lot* 2C **32**
Newtonairds. *Dum* 3D **13**
Newton Arlosh. *Cumb* 2B **8**
Newtongrange. *Midl* 3F **33**
Newtonhill. *Abers* 2E **61**
Newtonhill. *High* 1C **66**
**Newton Mearns**. *E Ren* 4D **31**
**Newtonmore**. *High* 2E **57**
Newton of Ardtoe. *High* 4F **53**
Newton of Balcanquhal. *Per* 2A **42**
Newton of Beltrees. *Ren* 4B **30**
Newton of Falkland. *Fife* 3B **42**
Newton of Mountblairy. *Abers* 4B **80**
Newton of Pitcairns. *Per* 2F **41**
Newton-on-the-Moor. *Nmbd* 4E **25**
Newton Reigny. *Cumb* 4D **9**
Newton Rigg. *Cumb* 4D **9**
Newton Stewart. *Dum* 1F **5**
Newton upon Ayr. *S Ayr* 3E **19**
New Town. *E Lot* 2A **34**
Newtown. *Abers* 3C **80**
Newtown. *Cumb* 3F **7**
(nr. Aspatria)
Newtown. *Cumb* 3E **9**
(nr. Brampton)
Newtown. *Cumb* 4E **9**
(nr. Penrith)
Newtown. *Falk* 1B **32**
Newtown. *High* 1A **56**
Newtown. *Nmbd* 3D **25**
Newtown. *Shet* 3G **101**
Newtown St Boswells. *Bord* 2E **23**
Newtyle. *Ang* 3B **50**
New Winton. *E Lot* 2A **34**
Niddrie. *Edin* 2F **33**
Niddry. *W Lot* 2C **32**
Nigg. *Aber* 1E **61**
Nigg. *High* 2F **77**
Nigg Ferry. *High* 3E **77**
Ninemile Bar. *Dum* 4D **13**
Nine Mile Burn. *Midl* 4D **33**
Nisbet. *Bord* 3F **23**
Nisbet Hill. *Bord* 4D **35**
Nitshill. *Glas* 3D **31**
Noness. *Shet* 4C **100**
Nonikiln. *High* 2D **77**
Nook. *Cumb* 4D **15**
Noranside. *Ang* 1D **51**
Norby. *Shet* 1A **100**
Norham. *Nmbd* 1C **24**
North Balfern. *Dum* 2F **5**
North Ballachulish. *High* 1B **46**
North Berwick. *E Lot* 1B **34**
North Charlton. *Nmbd* 3E **25**
North Collafirth. *Shet* 3F **101**
North Commonty. *Abers* 1D **71**
North Craigo. *Ang* 1F **51**
North Dronley. *Ang* 4C **50**
Northdyke. *Orkn* 1A **98**
North Erradale. *High* 1A **74**
North Fearns. *High* 2E **63**
North Feorline. *N Ayr* 3A **18**
Northfield. *Aber* 1D **61**
North Gluss. *Shet* 4F **101**
North Hazelrigg. *Nmbd* 2D **25**
North Kessock. *High* 1D **67**
North Middleton. *Midl* 4F **33**
North Middleton. *Nmbd* 3D **25**
Northmuir. *Ang* 2C **50**
North Murie. *Per* 1B **42**
North Ness. *Orkn* 3B **98**
North Port. *Arg* 1B **38**
North Queensferry. *Fife* 1D **33**
North Roe. *Shet* 3F **101**
North Ronaldsay Airport. *Orkn* 2H **99**
North Row. *Cumb* 4B **8**
North Sannox. *N Ayr* 1B **18**
North Shian. *Arg* 3A **46**
North Side. *Cumb* 4F **7**
North Sunderland. *Nmbd* 2F **25**
North Town. *Shet* 5B **100**
Northtown. *Orkn* 3C **98**
Northwall. *Orkn* 3H **99**
North Water Bridge. *Ang* 1F **51**
North Watten. *High* 2B **90**
Norwick. *Shet* 1H **101**
Noss. *Shet* 5B **100**
Nostie. *High* 3B **64**
Nunclose. *Cumb* 3D **9**
Nunnerie. *S Lan* 4E **21**
Nybster. *High* 1C **90**


## O


Oakbank. *Arg* 4E **45**
Oakbank. *W Lot* 3C **32**
Oakley. *Fife* 1C **32**
Oakshaw Ford. *Cumb* 4E **15**
Oape. *High* 3F **83**
Oathlaw. *Ang* 2D **51**
**Oban**. *Arg* **106** (1F **37**)
Oban. *W Isl* 2F **95**
Obsdale. *High* 3D **77**
Ochiltree. *E Ayr* 3A **20**
Ochtermuthill. *Per* 2D **41**
Ochtertyre. *Per* 1D **41**
Ockle. *High* 4E **53**
Octofad. *Arg* 4C **26**
Octomore. *Arg* 4C **26**
Oddsta. *Shet* 2H **101**
Odie. *Orkn* 5H **99**
Okraquoy. *Shet* 3C **100**
Old Aberdeen. *Aber* 1E **61**
Oldany. *High* 4C **86**
Old Bewick. *Nmbd* 3D **25**
Old Blair. *Per* 1D **49**
Old Bridge of Tilt. *Per* 1D **49**
Old Bridge of Urr. *Dum* 1C **6**
Old Dailly. *S Ayr* 2D **11**
Old Deer. *Abers* 1E **71**
Old Graitney. *Dum* 1C **8**
Oldhall. *High* 2B **90**
Oldhamstocks. *E Lot* 2D **35**
Old Kilpatrick. *W Dun* 2C **30**
Old Kinnernie. *Abers* 1C **60**
Oldmeldrum. *Abers* 3D **71**
Old Monkland. *N Lan* 3F **31**
Old Pentland. *Midl* 3E **33**
Old Philpstoun. *W Lot* 2C **32**
Old Rayne. *Abers* 3B **70**
Old Scone. *Per* 1A **42**
Oldshore Beg. *High* 2C **86**
Oldshoremore. *High* 2D **87**
Old Town. *Cumb* 3D **9**
Oldtown. *High* 1C **76**
Oldwall. *Cumb* 1D **9**
Old Westhall. *Abers* 3B **70**
Oldwhat. *Abers* 4D **81**
Olgrinmore. *High* 2F **89**
Ollaberry. *Shet* 3F **101**
Olrig. *High* 1A **90**
Omunsgarth. *Shet* 2B **100**
Onich. *High* 1B **46**
Onthank. *E Ayr* 2F **19**
Opinan. *High* 2A **74**
(nr. Gairloch)
Opinan. *High* 4A **82**
(nr. Laide)
Orasaigh. *W Isl* 1H **95**
Orbost. *High* 1B **62**
Ord. *High* 4F **63**
Ordale. *Shet* 1H **101**
Ordhead. *Abers* 4B **70**
Ordie. *Abers* 1F **59**
Ordiquish. *Mor* 4E **79**
Orgil. *Orkn* 2A **98**
Ormacleit. *W Isl* 4G **93**
Ormathwaite. *Cumb* 4B **8**
Ormiscaig. *High* 1B **74**
Ormiston. *E Lot* 3A **34**
Ormsaigbeg. *High* 1B **44**
Ormsaigmore. *High* 1B **44**
Ormsary. *Arg* 2B **28**
Orphir. *Orkn* 2B **98**
Orthwaite. *Cumb* 4B **8**
Orton. *Mor* 4E **79**
Osclay. *High* 4B **90**
Ose. *High* 1C **62**
Oskaig. *High* 2E **63**
Oskamull. *Arg* 4B **44**
Osmondwall. *Orkn* 4B **98**
Osnaburgh. *Fife* 2D **43**
Ospisdale. *High* 1E **77**
Otter Ferry. *Arg* 1D **29**
Otterswick. *Shet* 3H **101**
Oughterby. *Cumb* 2B **8**
Oughterside. *Cumb* 3A **8**
Oulton. *Cumb* 2B **8**
Ousby. *Cumb* 4F **9**
Ousdale. *High* 2F **85**
Outertown. *Orkn* 1A **98**
Overbister. *Orkn* 3H **99**
Over Finlarg. *Ang* 3D **51**
Overscaig. *High* 1F **83**
Overton. *Aber* 4D **71**
Overton. *High* 4B **90**
Overtown. *N Lan* 4A **32**
Oxgangs. *Edin* 3E **33**
Oxnam. *Bord* 4A **24**
Oxton. *Bord* 4A **34**
Oykel Bridge. *High* 3E **83**
Oyne. *Abers* 3B **70**


## P


Pabail Iarach. *W Isl* 3G **97**
Pabail Uarach. *W Isl* 3G **97**
Padanaram. *Ang* 2D **51**
Paddockhole. *Dum* 3B **14**
Paibeil. *W Isl* 1G **93**
(on North Uist)
Paibeil. *W Isl* 3E **95**
(on Taransay)
Paiblesgearraidh. *W Isl* 1G **93**
Pairc Shiaboist. *W Isl* 2D **96**
**Paisley**. *Ren* **107** (3C **30**)
Palgowan. *Dum* 3E **11**
Palnackie. *Dum* 2D **7**
Palnure. *Dum* 1F **5**
Panbride. *Ang* 4E **51**
Pannanich. *Abers* 2E **59**
Papa Stour Airport. *Shet* 1A **100**
Papa Westray Airport. *Orkn* 2F **99**
Papcastle. *Cumb* 4A **8**
Papigoe. *High* 2C **90**
Papil. *Shet* 3B **100**
Papple. *E Lot* 2B **34**
Pardshaw. *Cumb* 4F **7**
Park. *Abers* 2C **60**
Park. *Arg* 3A **46**
Park. *Dum* 2E **13**
Parkburn. *Abers* 2C **70**
Parkgate. *Cumb* 3B **8**
Parkgate. *Dum* 3E **13**
Parkhall. *W Dun* 2C **30**
Parkhead. *Cumb* 3C **8**
Parkhead. *Glas* 3E **31**
Parkneuk. *Abers* 4C **60**
Parkside. *N Lan* 4A **32**
Park Village. *Nmbd* 1F **9**
Parsonby. *Cumb* 4A **8**
Partick. *Glas* 3D **31**
Parton. *Cumb* 2B **8**
Parton. *Dum* 4B **12**
Pathhead. *Abers* 1F **51**
Pathhead. *E Ayr* 4B **20**
Pathhead. *Fife* 4B **42**
Pathhead. *Midl* 3F **33**
Path of Condie. *Per* 2F **41**
Pathstruie. *Per* 2F **41**
Patna. *E Ayr* 4F **19**
Pattiesmuir. *Fife* 1C **32**
Pawston. *Nmbd* 2B **24**
Paxton. *Bord* 4F **35**
Pearsie. *Ang* 2C **50**
Peaston. *E Lot* 3A **34**
Peastonbank. *E Lot* 3A **34**
Peathill. *Abers* 3E **81**
Peat Inn. *Fife* 3D **43**
Peaton. *Arg* 1A **30**
Peebles. *Bord* 1B **22**
Peel. *Bord* 2D **23**
Peinchorran. *High* 2E **63**
Peinlich. *High* 4D **73**
Pelutho. *Cumb* 3A **8**
Pencaitland. *E Lot* 3A **34**
**Penicuik**. *Midl* 3E **33**
Penifiler. *High* 1D **63**
Peninver. *Arg* 3E **17**
Penkill. *S Ayr* 2E **11**
Pennan. *Abers* 3D **81**
Pennyghael. *Arg* 1C **36**
Pennyvenie. *E Ayr* 1F **11**
Penpont. *Dum* 2D **13**
**Penrith**. *Cumb* 4E **9**
Penruddock. *Cumb* 4D **9**
Penston. *E Lot* 2A **34**
Perceton. *N Ayr* 1E **19**
Percyhorner. *Abers* 3E **81**
**Perth**. *Per* **107** (1A **42**)
Peterburn. *High* 1A **74**
Peterculter. *Aber* 1D **61**
**Peterhead**. *Abers* 1F **71**
Petertown. *Orkn* 2B **98**
Pettinain. *S Lan* 1E **21**
Pettycur. *Fife* 1E **33**
Philiphaugh. *Bord* 3D **23**
Philpstoun. *W Lot* 2C **32**
Pickletillem. *Fife* 1D **43**
Pierowall. *Orkn* 3F **99**
Pilton. *Edin* 2E **33**
Pinkerton. *E Lot* 2D **35**
Pinmore. *S Ayr* 2D **11**
Pinwherry. *S Ayr* 3C **10**
Piperhill. *High* 4F **77**
Pirnmill. *N Ayr* 1F **17**
Pisgah. *Stir* 3C **40**
Pitagowan. *Per* 1D **49**
Pitcairn. *Per* 2D **49**
Pitcairngreen. *Per* 1F **41**
Pitcalnie. *High* 2F **77**
Pitcaple. *Abers* 3C **70**
Pitcox. *E Lot* 2C **34**
Pitcur. *Per* 4B **50**
Pitfichie. *Abers* 4B **70**
Pitgrudy. *High* 4C **84**
Pitkennedy. *Ang* 2E **51**
Pitlessie. *Fife* 3C **42**
Pitlochry. *Per* 2E **49**
Pitmachie. *Abers* 3B **70**
Pitmaduthy. *High* 2E **77**
Pitmedden. *Abers* 3D **71**
Pitnacree. *Per* 2E **49**
Pitroddie. *Per* 1B **42**
Pitscottie. *Fife* 2D **43**
Pittentrail. *High* 3C **84**
Pittenweem. *Fife* 3E **43**
Pittulie. *Abers* 3E **81**
Pitversie. *Per* 2A **42**
Plaidy. *Abers* 4C **80**
Plains. *N Lan* 3F **31**
Plean. *Stir* 1A **32**
Plenmeller. *Nmbd* 1F **9**
Plockton. *High* 2B **64**
Plocrapol. *W Isl* 3F **95**
Plumbland. *Cumb* 4A **8**
Plumpton. *Cumb* 4D **9**
Plumpton Foot. *Cumb* 4D **9**
Plumpton Head. *Cumb* 4E **9**
Polbae. *Dum* 4D **11**
Polbain. *High* 3B **82**
Polbeth. *W Lot* 3C **32**
Polchar. *High* 1F **57**
Poles. *High* 4C **84**
Polglass. *High* 3B **82**
Polio. *High* 2E **77**
Polla. *High* 2E **87**
Polloch. *High* 1E **45**
Pollok. *Glas* 3D **31**
Pollokshaws. *Glas* 3D **31**
Pollokshields. *Glas* 3D **31**
Polmaily. *High* 2B **66**
**Polmont**. *Falk* 2B **32**
Polnessan. *E Ayr* 4F **19**
Polnish. *High* 3A **54**
Polskeoch. *Dum* 1B **12**
Polton. *Midl* 3E **33**
Polwarth. *Bord* 4D **35**
Ponton. *Shet* 1B **100**
Poolewe. *High* 1B **74**
Pooley Bridge. *Cumb* 4D **9**
Pool o' Muckhart. *Clac* 3F **41**
Porin. *High* 4A **76**
Portachoillan. *Arg* 4B **28**
Port Adhair Bheinn na Faoghla. *W Isl* 2G **93**
Port Adhair Thirlodh. *Arg* 3F **91**
Port Ann. *Arg* 1D **29**
Port Appin. *Arg* 3A **46**
Port Asgaig. *Arg* 3E **27**
Port Askaig. *Arg* 3E **27**
Portavadie. *Arg* 3D **29**
Port Bannatyne. *Arg* 3E **29**
Port Carlisle. *Cumb* 1B **8**
Port Charlotte. *Arg* 4C **26**
Port Driseach. *Arg* 2D **29**
Port Dundas. *Glas* 3D **31**
Port Ellen. *Arg* 1A **16**
Port Elphinstone. *Abers* 3C **70**
Portencalzie. *Dum* 4B **10**
Portencross. *N Ayr* 1C **18**
Port Erroll. *Abers* 2F **71**
Portessie. *Mor* 3F **79**
**Port Glasgow**. *Inv* 2B **30**
Portgordon. *Mor* 3E **79**
Portgower. *High* 2F **85**
Port Henderson. *High* 2A **74**
Portincaple. *Arg* 4D **39**
Portinnisherrich. *Arg* 2A **38**
Portknockie. *Mor* 3F **79**
Port Lamont. *Arg* 2E **29**
Portlethen. *Abers* 2E **61**
Portlethen Village. *Abers* 2E **61**
Portling. *Dum* 2D **7**
Port Logan. *Dum* 3B **4**
Portmahomack. *High* 1A **78**
Port Mholair. *W Isl* 3G **97**
Port Mor. *High* 4D **53**
Portnacroish. *Arg* 3A **46**
Portnahaven. *Arg* 4B **26**
Portnalong. *High* 2C **62**
Portnaluchaig. *High* 3F **53**
Portnancon. *High* 1F **87**
Port Nan Giuran. *W Isl* 3G **97**
Port nan Long. *W Isl* 5C **94**
Port Nis. *W Isl* 1G **97**
Portobello. *Edin* 2F **33**
Port of Menteith. *Stir* 3A **40**
Portormin. *High* 4A **90**
Portpatrick. *Dum* 2B **4**
Port Ramsay. *Arg* 3F **45**
Portree. *High* 1D **63**
Port Righ. *High* 1D **63**
Port Seton. *E Lot* 2A **34**
Portskerra. *High* 1D **89**
Portsonachan. *Arg* 1B **38**
Portsoy. *Abers* 3A **80**
Porttannachy. *Mor* 3E **79**
Portuairk. *High* 1B **44**
Port Wemyss. *Arg* 4B **26**
Port William. *Dum* 3E **5**
Potarch. *Abers* 2B **60**
Potterton. *Abers* 4E **71**
Poundland. *S Ayr* 3C **10**
Powburn. *Nmbd* 4D **25**
Powfoot. *Dum* 1A **8**
Powmill. *Per* 4F **41**
Prendwick. *Nmbd* 4D **25**
Pressen. *Nmbd* 2B **24**
Preston. *E Lot* 2B **34**
(nr. East Linton)
Preston. *E Lot* 2F **33**
(nr. Prestonpans)
Preston. *Nmbd* 3E **25**
Preston. *Bord* 4D **35**
Prestonmill. *Dum* 2E **7**
Prestonpans. *E Lot* 2F **33**
**Prestwick**. *S Ayr* 3E **19**
Priesthill. *Glas* 3D **31**
Priestland. *E Ayr* 2A **20**
Primsidemill. *Bord* 3B **24**
Prior Muir. *Fife* 2E **43**
Prospect. *Cumb* 3A **8**
Provanmill. *Glas* 3E **31**
Pulpit Hill. *Arg* 1F **37**
Pumpherston. *W Lot* 3C **32**


## Q


Quarrier's Village. *Inv* 3B **30**
Quarrywood. *Mor* 3C **78**
Quartalehouse. *Abers* 1E **71**
Quarter. *N Ayr* 3F **29**
Quarter. *S Lan* 4F **31**
Queenzieburn. *N Lan* 2E **31**
Quendale. *Shet* 5B **100**
Quholm. *Orkn* 1A **98**
Quilquox. *Abers* 2E **71**
Quindry. *Orkn* 3C **98**
Quothquan. *S Lan* 2E **21**
Quoyloo. *Orkn* 1A **98**
Quoyness. *Orkn* 2A **98**
Quoys. *Shet* 5G **101**
(on Mainland)
Quoys. *Shet* 1H **101**
(on Unst)


## R


Raby. *Cumb* 2A **8**
Rachan Mill. *Bord* 2A **22**
Racks. *Dum* 4F **13**
Rackwick. *Orkn* 3A **98**
(on Hoy)
Rackwick. *Orkn* 3F **99**
(on Westray)
Radernie. *Fife* 3D **43**
Rafford. *Mor* 4B **78**
Raggra. *High* 3C **90**
Raigbeg. *High* 3F **67**
Raise. *Cumb* 3F **9**
Rait. *Per* 1B **42**
Ralia. *High* 2E **57**
Ramasaig. *High* 1A **62**
Ramnageo. *Shet* 1H **101**
Ramsburn. *Mor* 4A **80**
Ramscraigs. *High* 1F **85**
Ramstone. *Abers* 4B **70**

PEFC Certified

This product is
from sustainably
managed forests and
controlled sources

PEFC/16-33-254    www.pefc.org

## SAFETY CAMERA INFORMATION

PocketGPSWorld.com's CamerAlert is a self-contained speed and red light camera warning system for SatNavs and Android or Apple iOS smartphones/tablets. Visit www.cameralert.com to download.

Safety camera locations are publicised by the Safer Roads Partnership which operates them in order to encourage drivers to comply with speed limits at these sites. It is the driver's absolute responsibility to be aware of and to adhere to speed limits at all times.

By showing this safety camera information it is the intention of Geographers' A-Z Map Company Ltd. to encourage safe driving and greater awareness of speed limits and vehicle speed. Data accurate at time of printing.